MW00619257

Praise for
The Art of Intimacy and the Hidden Challenge of Shame

Vick Kelly's *The Art of Intimacy and the Hidden Challenge of Shame* is an absolutely marvelous book. Dr. Kelly describes the foundation of human motivation – our feelings – and then uses his decades of clinical experience to show how shame can disrupt or save a marriage. This is the finest book available for therapists who work with couples and for couples who want to better understand and enhance their marriage and themselves.

—PAUL HOLINGER, M.D., M.P.H.
Dean, Chicago Institute for Psychoanalysis
Professor of Psychiatry, Rush University Medical Center
Author of *What Babies Say Before They Can Talk*
(Fireside, Simon & Schuster, 2003)

This book will be useful for a far broader audience than couples hoping to understand and improve the dynamics of their relationships. In the practice of Restorative Justice (an emerging field in criminal justice, school discipline, community, workplace and family relationships), wrongdoing is seen as a violation of people and relationships. Knowing more about shame is helping the restorative community reach a deeper understanding about the motivation for, and the impact, of crime and wrongdoing. Vick Kelly's book, in giving the restorative community a theory about the emotional dynamics of our relationships with each other, will help us improve our professional practice and our personal relationships.

—MARGARET THORSBORNE
Director, Margaret Thorsborne and Associates
Vice Chair of Restorative Practices International
Co-author of *Restorative Practice in Schools: Rethinking Behaviour Management*
(Inyahead Press, 2003)

"The best way to think about shame is that it is a message that contains very important information." With this simple statement, Vick Kelly sets the foundation for a perspective that will help every couple deal productively with the most powerful and potentially destructive force in their relationship—their capacity to feel shame. Kelly uncovers the widespread (though often invisible) influence of shame and helps us understand the nature of the emotion, the underlying affect that drives it, and how it penetrates intimate relationships.

I love this book for several reasons. Vick Kelly introduces the revolutionary new understanding of emotion contained in Affect Psychology. He is a marvel at getting to the heart of complicated ideas and using examples that bring them to life. Affect psychology is a form of self-knowledge, and Kelly makes himself accessible in the process of teaching. His open manner and wise voice help readers to see the unseeable and speak the unspeakable—to deal with their shame. He guides couples to *use* their shame instead of fearing it. The result is resilience—both individually and relationally. This book will benefit every couple; it should be required reading for engaging in relationships.

—DON R. CATHERALL, PH.D.
Professor of Clinical Psychiatry and Behavioral Sciences
Feinberg School of Medicine, Northwestern University
Author of *Emotional Safety: Viewing Couples Through the Lens of Affect* (Routledge, 2007)

The Art of Intimacy and the Hidden Challenge of Shame will be a powerful tool in the kit of any couple that wants to create and maintain a close and loving partnership. Dr. Kelly cuts through the clichés and gives us the science. He explains why we feel the way we do, and in turn how we behave in the relationships that matter the most; for better or for worse. Vick's writing is clear, caring and punctuated with wonderful anecdotes from a life rich in human connection.

—KATY HUTCHISON
Author of *Walking after Midnight*
(New Harbinger, 2006)

the ART of INTIMACY

and the
Hidden Challenge
of Shame

Vernon C. Kelly, Jr., M.D.

TOMKINS PRESS

ISBN: 978-1-936447-39-8

Produced by Maine Authors Publishing, Rockland, Maine
www.maineauthorspublishing.com

Printed in the United States of America

For Sharon

Sometimes hidden from me
in daily custom and trust,
so that I live by you unaware
as by the beating of my heart,

Suddenly you flare in my sight,
a wild rose blooming at the edge
of thicket, grace and light
where yesterday was only shade,

and once again I am blessed, choosing
again what I chose before.

—From "The Wild Rose"
by Wendell Berry

CONTENTS

Acknowledgments

Simply put: This book would never even have been conceived of had it not been for my mentor, colleague, and friend, Donald L. Nathanson, M.D. His prodding as my mentor, his brilliant insights as a colleague, and his unending support as my friend gave me the courage to step past the challenges of my own shame and expose my ideas about intimacy and shame. Thank you, Don, from the bottom of my heart!

Speaking of courage, I am deeply indebted to the many couples who have shared their stories with me over the years. I feel honored that they allowed me to see into their inmost selves as they strove to improve their ability to practice the art of intimacy. Their struggles often paralleled my own, and their insights always helped me improve my art.

To Gary David and Ron Denis, who read every word of my early manuscripts and offered suggestions, humor, and songs, I thank you for your cognitive abilities and the steadfastness of your friendships.

Thanks also go to special friends Nick and Jackie Scharff, Marg Thorsborne, Mick Brown, Peta Blood, Katy and Michael Hutchison, the hardworking Charles Gaby, and the marketing skills of Tom Hinkel, who helped me get my thick head past the original title that just didn't work.

To my colleagues Paul Holinger and Don Catherall, thank you for your generosity in sharing information about the world of publishing and for your brilliant books that make such good use of affect script psychology.

To the late Silvan S. Tomkins for his interest in hearing my ideas relating affect script psychology to intimate relationships, and, of course, for the stunning genius of his mind as he explored the question, What do human beings really want?, I offer thanks that I wish I could have given him while he was still with us.

To Wilson Brown, Bob Patrylo, Bob York, and CR my thanks for the many years of regular get-togethers on the first tee that, paradoxically, relieved the distress of writing while we practiced the art of golf with its not-so-hidden challenge of shame. And thanks also to Ronda Throne, C.M.T., and Austin Noonan, D.C., for their help keeping my back in shape to play golf; and also to Ed Lawlor and Pete for carrying the load.

To Jane, Genie, Colleen, David, Cheryl, and everyone associated with Maine Authors Publishing: Who knew that publishing one's book could be made so easy and so affordable? Thank you.

Besides my mother, father, and brothers, Fred and Greg, an understanding of the art of intimacy at the deepest levels of my heart and soul would have been impossible without the presence in my life of Molly, Hanna, Maddy, Collin, Louisa, and Katie. And I thank my lucky stars for the gifts of Chris Todd and Scott Sanoff. It would make all the hours of toil converting my ideas about the art of intimacy into written words worthwhile if Molly and Chris, Hanna and Scott gain a few tools from this book that enhance their own practice of the art of intimacy.

And last but really first: To my love, Sharon, whose grace, steadfastness, and work ethic put us all to shame—Here's looking at you, kid.

Preface

I suspect that you will enjoy this book far more than you expected. Even though its title momentarily focused your attention on the uncomfortable matter of shame, this is an engaging, remarkable, and fascinating story about some of the most common unpleasant experiences in our lives. Vick Kelly, a master psychiatrist who has always regarded the treatment of couples as the center of his career, insists that we recognize that people join together in intimate relationships to share such feelings as the pleasure of interpersonal safety, as well as the excitement of sexual interaction. Sure, the most passionate of courtships and the happiest of marriages must crash into discord from time to time, but we seek and strive for the most pleasant possible balance between these poles.

In contrast to the general mass of books and videos purporting to teach "anyone" how to assemble and maintain a "successful marriage," Dr. Kelly explains clearly and simply how a relationship forms, defines and names the forces that hold together or threaten a relationship, and what to do when nothing seems to work right. Rather than make everything seem obvious and "simple," he takes the reader along with him on a tour through the unnecessarily frightening world of human emotion in such a way that we find that when it comes to what does and doesn't work, we know far more than we thought. Different about his way of viewing couples is Vick Kelly's insistence that all of us must understand the real language of human emotion in order to build relationships that can withstand both the joys and pains of a normal marriage. All of us who've learned from him start using his ideas and language right after attending one of his public presentations.

Most of his colleagues have for years pestered him to do a series of videos about his work with couples, and he's always maintained that, independent of its unquestionable pleasures, marriage requires harder work if any couple is going to stick together through the squabbles that inevitably discolor our lives. He's written this book to convince the reader that all of us have a lot to learn about ourselves, about each other, and about what makes marriage work. I wish I could look over your shoulders as you read this fascinating book, and I know you'll be glad that you did.

I've spent several decades trying to understand why we humans experience emotion, what purpose it serves in normal life, how from time to time we are thrown into confusion by the occasional explosions of our own emotions experienced in situations that caught us unawares, and how we are affected by the intense, apparently uncontrolled emotion of others. I'd come to understand that tranquilizers helped us control emotions that we were otherwise unable to modulate. Using this kind of logic, depression was easy to understand as the inability to modulate painful emotions like sadness or gloom, and the antidepressants seemed to help us reestablish whatever balance of pleasant and unpleasant emotions made us more comfortable.

I'd written a lot about what we psychiatrists call the "shame family of emotions"—painful feelings ranging from slight decreases in self-esteem (our appraisal of ourselves) to emotional pain so horrific that people sometimes preferred to die rather than experience it anymore. As I studied these emotions, most episodes of rage, fury, explosions of temper, throwing things around the room until the rage seemed to decrease, and physical attacks on other people turned out to be reactions to shame that felt so awful and made such individuals feel helpless, worthless, and utterly incompetent unless or until they could become "powerful" by terrifying someone else into submission or utter helplessness. I came to understand that, for many people, ordinary alcoholic beverages were capable of reducing the pain of shame to such a degree that these folks learned to live with alcohol as either their personal tranquilizer or the elixir that could turn them from shame-ridden, helpless adults into raging monsters who felt competent only when the subjects of their rage had themselves been humiliated. The study of shame allowed me to understand a great deal that had been left out of my professional training, and I spent many years explaining to my professional colleagues what I had learned about this previously ignored emotion.

Throughout several decades of such work, Dr. Kelly was both a partner in my work on these puzzles and a remarkably talented designer of ways to help people gain control of their shame-based rage. He and I lectured together on many occasions, and we organized large meetings in which we taught our colleagues how to operationalize the concepts we'd developed. Yet there was one significant difference in our approach to the management of shame: my focus started and remained on the internal life of individual adults, and Dr. Kelly became intensely interested in the way the personal shame of one individual could affect the emotional life of that person's "significant other." For all of us who "do psychotherapy," Kelly showed that the way each person handles his or her shame within the borders of an intimate relationship was a major factor in the degree of intimacy possible for that couple, and the degree of safety that might be experienced by both partners.

This book, then, is his conversation with the reader. It explains Dr. Kelly's long-studied and quite inspiring ways of teaching people how to deal with their own shame in ways that produced the least amount of damage to their intimate others. His ability to find humor in some of the most difficult situations imaginable will both amuse and enlighten you. He'll tell you about the strategies he's devised to help people out of shame-based binds that so often trap couples in fights that seem to go on forever.

In other words, I rather think that anyone who has ever tried and failed to manage an intimate relationship will enjoy this book. People who've survived a divorce will shake their heads as they come to understand what no one had ever explained before. Men and women, gay couples, senior citizens who have nearly given up any hope of changing what appears to be an unchangeable spouse, teachers who feel helpless with students who become explosive for no obvious reason, parents who feel unable to explain the complaints of their adolescent children, dating couples who wonder why their significant other seems to refuse any attempt to talk about "what went wrong," and so on. The list can go on and on, for these shame-based conflicts are for many people the bane of their existence, the social traps from which they have never been able to escape. This, then, is your book, and I hope you enjoy learning from Vick Kelly, my distinguished colleague and closest friend, known on the title page of this book as Vernon C. Kelly, Jr., M.D. Read, learn, enjoy.

Don Nathanson
Wynnewood, PA
February 2011

Introduction

This is a book about the feelings that lead to success or failure in relationships. Based on my experience working with couples since the late 1960s, and the findings from the psychology of affect and script originated by Silvan S. Tomkins and furthered by Donald Nathanson, I have concluded that *hidden shame* is the primary reason once close intimate relationships fail, and that shame is the leading cause of divorce.

That this is so is counterintuitive and hidden from most people in Western culture for a number of reasons. Perhaps the most significant is the generally held belief that the word *shame* means only that one has done something to be "ashamed of." I have devoted Chapter 2 to a discussion of the shame family of emotions in order to demonstrate that the inborn capacity to experience shame leads—in addition to feeling ashamed—to a varied and complex group of emotions.

Secondly, Western culture focuses more on behavior than on the feelings that motivate behavior. Because of this, what we usually encounter when studying the reasons that relationships fail is a list of behaviors. This list includes such items as infidelity; inability to communicate; inability to agree on important issues like money and sex; lack of commitment to the relationship; failed expectations; physical, sexual or emotional abuse; alcoholism and other addictions; growing apart because of a change in priorities; and falling out of love. Thinking only of specific behaviors as the reason a relationship fails rather than of the feelings that motivate the behaviors is backwards. It is an artifact of early explorations into human psychology based on the false belief (or perhaps the wish) that man alone is THE rational mammal on planet Earth. Therefore, grounded as they were in this belief, early psychologists explained feelings as aberrations that only arose in crisis situations or in the mentally infirm. They were severely limited in their ability to explain human motivation because they had no good theory about how normal feelings arose.

Appendix I is "A Primer of Affect Psychology." This is a partial summary of the original work of Silvan S. Tomkins. In my opinion, Tomkins described the most complete and compelling theory of how affects, feelings, and emotions arise as a normal part of our biology. To understand better my perspective on how feelings motivate relationships, I suggest you read the Primer and/or go to the Tomkins Institute website at www.tomkins.org where following the link Affect/Script Psychology will provide you with further readings and articles to study.

Thirdly, shame is such a negative feeling that a patient once said to me, "I hate that word *shame*. Can't we call it Harvey or something?" She is not alone in her desire to avoid saying the word shame out loud, or even thinking about it for that matter. It is a difficult word for everyone because it conjures up too many negative experiences and feelings that most of us would rather forget, especially since the memory of those events often recreates the sense of helplessness or feelings of inferiority we had at that time. Tomkins wrote that negative affects—wired into our brains before birth—are inherently punishing. It is part of our nature to want them to stop. Since shame can range from the slightly unpleasant experience of mild embarrassment to the deepest depths of humiliation and mortification, nobody would consciously want to relive such feelings.

And finally, the defenses all of us erect to protect us from the shame experience obscure shame and hide from us the prevalence of shame in causing the dissolution of relationships. Every one of the "reasons" or "behaviors" for relational distress listed above is a cause of shame and can by caused by shame. Chapter 6 outlines the specific patterns of defense that lead to the behaviors found in that list. Donald Nathanson first described these patterns in his 1992 seminal work, *Shame and Pride: Affect, Sex, and the Birth of the Self.* My insights into intimacy success and failure are a direct extension of the discoveries elucidated in that book by my friend and colleague decades ago.

Despite the power of shame to destroy relationships, it is my happy task—and the major focus of this book—to inform you about another side of shame, a side that makes it one of the most powerful and potentially useful features of our biologic makeup. In this regard, I would compare shame to our immune system—a system that usually operates completely outside of our awareness, removing dangerous viruses, bacteria, and toxins from our bodies. At other times, however, immune reactions cause symptoms that we become painfully aware of. They can be minor things that range from a mild sore throat, achiness, and slight fever to serious incapacitation from high fever and the inability to get out of bed. Furthermore, the immune system has an extremely toxic side. It can turn against the body and cause terrible chronic illnesses such as lupus erythematosus, rheumatoid arthritis, Crohn's disease, type I diabetes, multiple sclerosis, and ulcerative colitis, to mention just a few.

Like the immune system, shame's normal, out of awareness (unconscious) function in adults allows us, among other things, to live harmoniously in dyadic personal relationships, families, and society because we care about how we come across to others. This is in dramatic contrast to isolated cases of shamelessness which present a serious problem in all cultures. Imagine what a disaster it would be for human societies if no one had a sense of shame. People might go around spitting on anyone they didn't like or making rude, nasty comments about the noses, bodies, faces, skin color, and other traits of ordinary folks. Instead, for the most part, the adults in our culture experience shame if they treat others that way and therefore avoid doing it. This is normal healthy shame guiding us toward civilized interaction.

However, even in civilized gatherings, we become aware of mild shame reactions at times when we put our foot in our mouth or forget to do something we promised we would do or mistakenly greet a stranger thinking they are someone we know. Such shame reactions are like the mild sore throat. The more serious shame reactions occur when we feel rejected or hurt by someone, or when we do something really dumb at work that gets us fired. Such things can be incapacitating, making us want to avoid people and never leave the house. And, like the immune system, some shame states can develop into chronically toxic reactions when the intensity becomes so great that one feels deeply humiliated to the point of mortification—a feeling state that can cause deep depression, suicide, or murderous rage to the point of homicide.

Perhaps the most important objective of this book is to expose the positive function of shame so the reader can see that—not unlike our immune system—

*Shame is a powerful **gift** we have inherited that can help us keep our intimate relationships happy, healthy, and loving.*

However, also paralleling our immune system's capabilities:

Shame is so powerful, it inevitably destroys intimacy if we do not use its information properly.

On another note, I need to add that this book about relationships is unlike most others. The difference is that it provides you with a new biological and psychological framework that emphasizes the *similarities* between men and women, unlike others that focus on the *differences* between the sexes. Here I offer an option other than the currently popular myth that women and men are permanently alien to one another, or that because of the "difference" in the way men and women express emotion, there is an unbridgeable gulf between them.

You can cavort with the members of your sex and insist "I'll never understand women" or "I'll never understand men." *And you never will.* Or you can challenge these culturally reinforced beliefs. You can withdraw from the war between the sexes and follow the advice of the military computer WOPR in the movie *War Games.* After a survey of all possible nuclear war outcomes, the computer concluded: "Strange game, Professor Falken. The only way to win is not to play." If you chose this option, then what is written here will help you probe beneath the differences that feed the women versus men war and learn about a basic human endowment that renders women and men more alike than different.

Those who believe the myth that women are too emotional and men are too logical have apparently never seen a man yell at his television set when a basketball official makes a bad call, or watched men ranting and raving in the stands at a football game. Nor have they observed the reaction of deep shame and hurt in a man recently jilted by his girlfriend. And those who think women are incapable of logical thinking have been living under a rock. They have missed the contributions to the world by women like Marie Curie, Hilary Clinton, Eleanor Roosevelt, Dorothy Mary Crowfoot Hodgkin, Pearl Buck, Margaret Mead, Billie Jean King, and Margaret Thatcher, to name a tiny percentage of those whose ability to be logical has advanced medicine, politics, cultural understanding, literature, and sports. (One of my personal favorites is golfing great Annika Sorenstam, who logically charted every single shot she ever made during golf tournaments in order to understand where she needed to improve.)

During almost four decades treating troubled couples, it has been my impression that when people lose sight of their similarities, things get worse. In troubled times, knowing about our differences is not very helpful.

Intimacy troubles are about not *feeling* good about one another; not *feeling* close, not *feeling* emotionally connected, not *feeling* like allies, *feeling* angry at each other, and *feeling* hurt by the other. All of us have these feelings. They may be triggered by different things and at different levels of intensity, but they are the same feelings in both partners.

And from the perspective of what men and women alike really want from an emotionally intimate relationship? They want to *feel* good, *feel* like friends and allies, *feel* that they can trust the other not to hurt them, *feel* that someone is interested in their welfare and enjoys the interest of another in them. All of us have these feelings, too. They may be triggered by different things and at different levels of intensity, but they are the same feelings in both partners.

The biological reality about the inborn, innate affect **shame**, a reality equally distributed between men and women, is that: **shame never happens unless there are positive feelings that precede it**. That this is so is one of the basic tenets of *affect psychology*, the most basic building block of Tomkins's Human Being Theory. Its introduction in the early 1960s in volumes I and II of his magnum opus, *Affect Imagery Consciousness*, brought about no fanfare whatsoever, in spite of its being the first theory of human motivation to include all the genetic, biologic, cognitive, and psychological discoveries of the time. The density of Tomkins's writing style and his lack of the political savvy of empire builders like Freud buried his work in relative obscurity. Almost all of the very few who did catch on and began to employ his work had been his students.

The breadth of Tomkins's knowledge was astounding. He knew about and understood not only the psychology of the Freudians and many others, but also physics, brain and body physiology, philosophy, politics, history, artificial intelligence, evolution, literature, addiction, biblical scripture, and more. I was not surprised to learn that he had majored in playwriting, philosophy, and psychology at the University of Pennsylvania in his personal quest to answer the question: "What do human beings really want?"

My private practice in psychiatry and my own personal growth and capacity for intimacy began a complete overhaul not long after my introduction to affect psychology. The first change I made was to begin teaching the basics of affect psychology to all my patients. I believe it is senseless for a therapist who has studied human psychology for years to leave patients or clients guessing about their emotions and motivations. I want people to have a simple, straightforward language with which to communicate with themselves, their significant others, and me. While I have attempted to capture the essence of this teaching in Appendix I, throughout the book, I make reference to affects, feelings, and emotions to reinforce how we can become more aware of our innermost selves—a critical step in the development of a strong capacity for emotional intimacy.

My reward for inculcating affect psychology into my work has been a remarkable transformation in the efficiency of psychotherapy. It has also become much easier to understand the ebb and flow of negative emotions that require treatment with psychopharmacologic interventions. The ability of my patients to identify changes in emotion—positive and negative—makes treatment by psychotherapy or the use of medication a simpler task. This is better for them and better for me. My punishment is that so many people have asked me to write down what I have taught them verbally, I would feel embarrassed if I did not make the effort, even though writing is not my first language; after all, I majored in chemistry!

It is important for you to understand that affect psychology is a complete shift from the way one usually thinks about emotion. Most academic or word-of-mouth teaching about human emotion and motivation is missing vital components. Furthermore, shame over our lifetime for being "too emotional" forces us to reduce our awareness of something we knew intimately as kids—how we felt. If, therefore, the language and theories presented herein feel somewhat alien, do not be surprised. It has taken some of the greatest minds I've ever known quite some time to grasp the apparently simple fact that innate, inborn affect motivates all aspects of human behavior.

An apologia: I have written this book knowing I would have to avoid a great deal of data about personality, personality formation, and various biological complexities and differences between men and women. I did so in order to highlight the specific features of shame and how this affect influences and teaches us something very useful about managing our intimate relationships. One might justifiably accuse me of being overly simplistic because of this decision. But the other side of the coin is that those who are overly complex create the illusion for both their readers and themselves that they "really" understand what motivates us. I insist that such "experts" are deluding themselves. There is no such thing as "complete" knowledge of virtually anything, especially human personality and motivation, which have roots in incompletely understood biology, evolution, and social and personal history, not to mention the things that happen to us daily. It is a feature of our cognitive system to want to understand everything; unfortunately, this leads many to believe that they understand more than they really do because of what they don't know they don't know.

The relationship focus of this book is on any two people motivated by powerful positive feelings to make a long-term emotional commitment to one another. (Disclaimer: I am a product of Western culture. I have only worked with couples from that culture. I have not studied or been otherwise exposed to intimate relationships and marriages in Eastern cultures. I have no doubt shame is a prominent feature of troubled relationships in those cultures also, but I have no direct knowledge about it.) I present the simplified version of the motivational basis for relationships from the perspective of affect psychology in Chapter 3. From there through Chapter 8, I discuss the effects of shame—both positive and negative—on a couple's emotional connection. In Chapters 9 and 10, I suggest a path for the maximizing of positive feelings and the minimizing of negative feelings in relationships, using the powerful message provided by shame. I discovered the suggested path only because of the privilege granted me by so many couples to stumble along with them in a journey toward happiness. I thank them all.

Chapters 11 and 12 are necessarily incomplete. Relationship problems caused by sexually generated shame or the potential shame inherent in biological illnesses deserve a great deal of attention. For now, that attention must wait until another time.

And finally, while this is not a book about love, I hope it will illuminate some aspects of love. My image of love is akin to the giant tapestry I once saw covering an entire section of a large wall at the Philadelphia Museum of Art. When standing on the other side of the room, one can get a feel for the entire piece but not understand all of its intricate parts. When standing very close, one can understand the intricate parts but not get a feel for the entire piece. Hopefully, I have exposed some aspects of human motivation that make love possible; for it is love, after all, that made this book possible.

CHAPTER 1

The Art of Intimacy

D isclaimer 1: this is not a book about SEX—although I harbor no personal objections to sex if you engage in it safely and with someone you love and trust. This is a book about *emotional intimacy*, especially that which involves a significant other in your life with whom you feel a deep, long-term commitment, and sex is only one part of that story.

Disclaimer 2: this is not a book about intimacy as defined by philosophers, poets, or romantic novelists. This is a book about ordinary people like you and me struggling with everyday issues and personal vulnerabilities that interfere with our ability to remain close to and feel warm and snuggly with our significant other.

Below I present four scenarios representative of the commonplace issues I intend to address in order to help you better understand and deal with what goes wrong and what goes right in your emotionally intimate relationships. At some point, I will also discuss issues with somewhat more dramatic emotional impact, but in my experience, the daily little things that interfere with our relationships, because they occur more frequently than the big things and are often, therefore, likely to be ignored, can have a greater negative impact on emotional intimacy.

Final Disclaimer: the names and identities of all the people mentioned in this book are disguised to protect their privacy. Wherever I have by chance picked two names of a real-life couple, the story is not about them. (I will explain the lettering for the scenarios in Chapter 6.)

Scenario AO:

Tom was very distressed about how grumpy he was with Alice. Everything was going so well. Their three-month-old son was healthy, happy, and sleeping through the night almost all the time. And Tom had finally received the big promotion and with it a substantial raise that virtually put an end to their worries about money. At first, he thought his grumpiness and snapping at Alice had something to do with the several months' interruption in their sex life occasioned by some difficulty toward the end of her pregnancy and then the prohibition on sex until she fully healed from her vaginal delivery. But Alice had seduced him back to bed when little Tommy was two months old, and their sex life now seemed better than ever. And yet he still found himself snapping at her and being overly critical of things she did. This was a complete change in his behavior. It puzzled him how he could have once been so adoring of Alice, only now to find himself being such a jerk to her.

Scenario AS:

Everybody said Mindy and Matthew were a perfect match. She was beautiful, outgoing, and gregarious, while he was handsome and the strong, silent type. Because he seldom initiated conversation, she'd had some moments of doubt about the relationship when they were courting. However, she readily accepted his marriage proposal because his warmth, tenderness, and cheerful demeanor when they were alone made her feel wonderful and deeply loved. Before they were married, she had always been able to get him to share his deepest feelings, hopes, and dreams, but things changed when he opened his business. Even though his office was in their home, it became rare for them to have deep conversations. She knew he was busy and excited about their prospects for the future, but his feelings seemed more and more of a mystery to her. She began to question herself and wonder what she was doing wrong. She had put on a couple of pounds since they were married. Did he find her gross and disgusting? He had gone to a better college than she, and he never seemed to pay attention to ideas she had about his business. Did he think she was stupid? She was often disorganized, while he was super organized and always had his things neatly in place. Did he think she was incompetent? She noticed that now she would often put herself down when speaking to him, even though he never criticized anything she said.

Scenario W:

Sally and Sarah had lived together for fifteen years. The relationship that had begun as a steamy affair when both were on the rebound so many years before had settled into a gentle, loving, and supportive union that surprised both of them. The battles that plagued the first years of their life together seldom occurred any more. The couples therapist they worked with for several years had helped them manage that part of their relationship. They often joked that they were now the "S's squared," Sally and Sarah, Safe and Secure. But over the past six months, Sarah had found herself strangely withdrawn. It reminded her of how she had been around her family when she was a teenager struggling with feelings about her sexual orientation. Sally did not seem any different to her, except that Sally's job had become more demanding. Sally often came home very late at night, too tired to do much of anything but have a quick dinner and then head straight to bed. Sarah was happy for Sally because Sally felt greatly fulfilled by her new responsibilities, and they both enjoyed the increased income. Sarah knew she should say something to Sally about what she was feeling, but she just could not bring herself to do it. It would upset Sally too much. She kept her thoughts to herself and, more and more often, begged off of sex when Sally approached her, claiming she did not feel well.

Scenario A:

Betty and Harry were finally in decent shape economically. They had gone through many ups and downs with money while helping put their three kids through college. But now they had almost paid off the mortgage, and their credit card debt was negligible. They were really enjoying their time alone together. For them the empty nest syndrome was one wherein they found the greatest closeness they had experienced since before the birth of their first child. Harry was not a big drinker; in fact, his friends called him a "lightweight" whenever he went out with them because he got tipsy on just a couple of beers. This is why it was so troubling to both Betty and Harry that he seemed to get drunk almost every time her family came to visit for a few days. The most he ever drank when he and Betty were alone was one beer, as did she. Her family had been extremely helpful with extra gifts of money for the kids when they were in college. They had always loved Harry and had been thrilled when he and Betty got married. They were not big drinkers, but they always brought beer with them when they visited, and each night while they were there,

Harry had more than a few and passed out in his chair.

Did you recognize something about you or your relationship in any of these brief vignettes? All four of these couples were in relationships and life circumstances that were essentially favorable. Their emotional intimacy was, for the most part, good, and all four couples remained together long after they sought therapy.

Each, however, was experiencing some form of interference with their emotional intimacy that created a problem. While the art of intimacy may be difficult to define, it certainly must include notions about being warm, close, and feeling as if the other is interested in you and your feelings. To paraphrase an old saying, "I may not know how to define the art of intimacy, but I sure know what it feels like." It feels good. But since interference with those good feelings must inevitably occur, the definition also has to include something about the ability of two people to recognize when it feels bad and to develop some proficiency in correcting whatever is wrong.

That is where shame comes in!

Shame is the hidden element in each of the four scenarios presented above. Unless you already know a great deal about the dynamics of shame, I suspect that, except perhaps in Mindy's case, you are at a loss to identify the presence of shame in these relationships. I assure you it is present, hidden behind the defensive behaviors of the people involved. Tom's anger and criticism, Mindy's self-doubts, Sarah's withdrawal, and Harry's drinking are all shame-related defenses. Each is a behavior resulting from the need to defend against vulnerable feelings. And each behavior makes things worse.

As you will learn in this book, the hidden challenge of shame is twofold. First off, it is hidden. Secondly, it makes things worse. However—and the most salient motive behind my writing of this book—shame is also an invaluable tool. It carries a message that is the key to developing true proficiency in the art of intimacy.

We will revisit the four couples later on to see exactly where and why the shame is hidden. But first things first: If you are like most people, my use of the word *shame* is likely to be troubling. In the next chapter, I will attempt to expand your thinking about shame so that we can move beyond the notion that the word only means someone has done something to be "ashamed of."

One final thought about the art of intimacy: the artistry involved in creating and maintaining an emotionally intimate relationship is a highly individual phenomenon. Every individual brings unique skills, strengths, and weaknesses to their intimate relationship. Each couple evolves special ways of relating to each other based on the interaction of these unique characteristics. I encourage all couples to read and learn as much as they can about emotional intimacy to enhance their skills. But the bottom line is that only you and your partner know what it is like to be with one another. I intend to give you my perspectives on emotional intimacy and how shame influences it. However, since only you really know what you feel, I respectfully leave it to you to paint the picture of emotional intimacy that works for you.

CHAPTER 2

The Shame Family of Emotions

One day early in my career as an aspiring amateur golfer, I threw a golf club that barely missed bashing in the head of one of my playing partners. After the moment of fear that I might have killed him passed, I felt terribly ashamed. Later that day, I mentioned the episode to the golf club's head professional, Ted McKenzie. I sought any advice he might have to help me deal with my anger when things did not go well on the golf course. (I had no idea at the time that shame, not anger, was the real problem.) He said that he too had had difficulty controlling his impulse to throw clubs until the day an incident took place that virtually eliminated his club-throwing from then on. He was playing in a professional tournament when he missed making a very short putt. He tapped in the remaining putt, and, as he walked off the green, launched his putter skyward. It landed squarely on the roof of a nearby maintenance shed. Upon deciding he could not finish the tournament without his putter, he borrowed a ladder and, as an amused gallery looked on, climbed up to retrieve it, his face red with embarrassment.

I doubt there is anyone reading this who cannot recall some incident where they felt similarly embarrassed or ashamed, whether it was because of something they did or something they said. Feeling ashamed of oneself is not only a common experience, it is also the first thing people think of when the word *shame* is mentioned. However, research into shame has discovered that feeling ashamed is only one member of a very large family of emotions made possible by the human ability to experience shame. Furthermore, that same research has made it clear that as bad as the moment of feeling ashamed can be, and as destructive as its effects can be, it also can be an extraordinarily positive force in the lives of individuals, couples, families, and communities.

That shame significantly reduced the club-throwing of my golf professional is a positive outcome of his embarrassing episode. (Later on, I will describe my discoveries about shame that significantly altered my own "anger" on the golf course.) On a much larger and more significant scale, I think you would agree that if we lived in an entirely "shameless" society, our lives would be much more unpleasant. What, for instance, would it be like if shame did not prevent people from spitting on us in the street just because they did not like the way we looked? Or if shame did not stop people from commenting on every physical imperfection they see in us—"Wow, that giant blemish on your forehead is really ugly"?

It is because of our inborn ability to feel shame that parents are able to mold children into good citizens who show respect for others. Without shame, it would be impossible for human beings to live together with any degree of comfort. Indeed, the individual acts of shamelessness we learn about from news reports appall most of us and make us wonder how anyone could treat other people that way. The vast majority of citizens could never have done what Bernard Madoff did, shamelessly cheating trusting clients out of millions of dollars, eventually ruining the lives of many people, and even seriously damaging the integrity of a number of charitable trusts.

The positive effects of shame are only possible because it feels so awful that we are strongly motivated to avoid it. The experience of shame or feeling ashamed triggers a standard, universally recognizable, and most unpleasant set of thoughts and feelings. We want to climb into a hole in the ground and disappear; we feel dumb; we feel like no one could love us because we are a defective, incompetent, stupid idiot with no redeeming features to have said or done whatever it was that made us feel ashamed and exposed us to everyone else. And the physiological effects of shame make it worse because we feel even more ashamed—ashamed of being ashamed—if people see our red, flushed face in the seconds or minutes after the triggering of shame causes us to blush.

I doubt that anything I've written so far is news to you. Feeling ashamed is a common experience and the first thing people think of when they hear the word *shame*. But have you ever thought about where shame comes from? How come human beings can feel ashamed? Are we born with shame, or does it only develop later in life when we can understand the words and body language of those we grow up around? In other words, is it simply a learned behavioral reaction? The answer to this last question surprised me at first. Shame is *both* an inborn, innate physiologic reaction and a learned response! Actually, this is logical. How could we simply *learn* to have shame if we did not have some predisposition for it? It is somewhat analogous to fear responses. How could we learn fight or flight if we did not have a predisposition, something inborn, that would motivate the learning of such behaviors?

The Origins of Shame

The innate, inborn predisposition that becomes shame is just one of a series of nine such capabilities that humans have evolved. They are called *affects*. Each of the nine affects is present virtually from birth. They are the precursors of our feelings. In other words, it is only because we are born with affects that we become capable of having feelings and emotions. In his book *What Babies Say Before They Can Talk*, Paul Holinger beautifully describes the earliest expression of the nine affects in infants, stressing that it is through the affects that babies communicate their feelings even before any learning has taken place. (Dr. Holinger's book is a must-read for new parents interested in understanding and maximizing emotional connection with their infants.)

Each of the nine affects is a separate, completely biological, unconscious mechanism—not unlike a knee-jerk response—triggered when a specific pattern of sensory information from either outside or inside our body registers in our brain. The sensory information can include things we see, hear, smell, taste, touch, or feel inside of us like hunger, pain, and sexual feelings. When an affect is triggered, we become consciously aware of whatever it was that triggered it. In fact, we **only become consciously aware of things if an affect is triggered**, which makes affect the most critical element in human motivation; after all, you cannot be motivated by something unless and until you become aware of it.

Each affect has, as part of its mechanism of action, unique facial and body language responses that make it easy for us to recognize them and distinguish them from one another. The other affects besides shame are interest, enjoyment, surprise, fear, distress, anger, disgust, and dissmell (the response to foul smells). In Appendix I, "A Primer of Affect Psychology," I go into much greater detail, including pictures demonstrating the facial signals, about the evolved, biological function of our brain's *affect system*. If you choose to read it now, you will have a better understanding of what is to follow. However, it is not absolutely necessary to read it if the three preceding paragraphs are clear to you, and if you keep in mind the following:

1. Each of the nine affects has the evolved function of giving us very specific information about the sensory information that triggers it. For example, interest lets us know something pleasant is happening, distress tells us too much unpleasant stuff is going on for too long, fear signals that too much is happening too fast, and so on.
2. When we become aware of an affect, it is called a *feeling*.
3. As we progress from infancy to adulthood, our individually unique experience and learning from those around us gradually molds our feelings into what we call *emotions*. Because all of our personal experiences—our biographies—are different, we all seem very different emotionally. However,
4. all the feelings and emotions that you have ever had or heard about originate from the nine innate affects or from combinations of two or more of them.

In this last respect, I liken the affect *shame* to wheat grain. You may or may not think of wheat when you eat bread, cookies, breakfast cereal, pasta, noodles, or couscous, or when you drink beer and other alcohols or when you look at roofing thatch or even when you consider biofuels. And yet wheat is the basic element that must be present for any of these materials to exist. Likewise, you probably do not think very often of shame as the origin of such feelings as abandonment, despair, sadness, rejection, loneliness, isolation, hurt, shyness, frustration, or even the currently popular notion of "disrespecting" someone. On the other hand, you may well see shame at the heart of a number of traits that appear in some personalities, such as inferiority, low self-esteem, alienation, and defenses like bitter sarcasm, machoism, self put-downs, withdrawal, drug abuse, perfectionism, workaholism, the compulsion to accumulate vast amounts of wealth, the compulsion to have multiple plastic surgeries to try to make the face and body look perfect, or in people who you think of as having a "big ego." Shame is the origin of all of these defenses and personality traits and many, many more aspects of humans, including how relationships form and then either succeed or fail. How all of this is so should become more evident when we consider the function of the inborn, innate affect shame.

The Function of Shame

It is most useful to think of the affect system in our brain as a mechanism that gives us information about things by making us feel either good or bad. We feel good when it creates the affects of interest or enjoyment. We feel bad when it creates the affects of fear, distress, anger, disgust, dissmell, or shame. Because we feel good or bad, we are motivated to do something. For instance, if something or someone is triggering fear, distress, anger, disgust, or dissmell, we feel bad and try to stop or get away from those things or people. Likewise, if we are interested in or enjoying things, we feel good and want to keep on doing those things.

What if something happens that gets in the way of our being able to do the things that give us interest or enjoyment? Obviously, the wiring in our brains makes us feel bad whenever that happens. As surprising as it may sound at first, *shame* evolved to give us the information that something has intervened and is preventing us from feeling good. Shame is the unpleasant signal that good things have been stopped. This is a vitally important piece of information. There would be no way to manage the feeling-good part of our lives if we never got the message that something was preventing us from feeling that way. It is the evolved function of shame to give us that information. (Please note carefully that "good things being stopped without us wanting them to be" is very different from our simply having lost interest in or the enjoyment of something. If we have lost interest in something, then there is no interest present to be blocked, and no triggering of shame occurs.)

Why did Silvan Tomkins, the first person to describe the affect system, give the name **shame-humiliation** to the affect triggered when there is an impediment to one of the positive affects? The simple answer is that he paid very careful attention to and did research looking at the faces of thousands of people, and he saw them consistently react with shame when either interest or enjoyment was blocked. This was a very complex task because of all of the ways humans disguise or defend against shame in order to stop the unpleasant feeling. Furthermore, all of us have shame about having shame, so it is only logical that we learn to do many things to hide it from ourselves and others. (If you have not yet read "A Primer of Affect Psychology" in Appendix I, now might be a good time to read the final section about shame affect.)

✦ **CRITICAL POINT: The evolved function of shame affect is to give us information that some impediment has gotten in the way of our experiencing interest or enjoyment.**

The best way to think about shame is that it is a message that contains very important information. Even though it feels bad, shame alerts us to blockages or impediments to our good feelings. The biggest problem with shame when it comes to intimate relationships is that it involves bad feelings, and, naturally, that creates the tendency in all of us to hide from or ignore it. My primary goal for this book is to increase your awareness of when and where to find shame in interpersonal relationships so that you can use shame's information to help restore the positive feelings and reasons you have for wanting to be in these relationships. In my clinical work over the last four decades, I have observed that when people do not know anything about shame, it leads to negative shame spirals (see Chapter 8) that destroy relationships in families, couples, and communities.

That Tomkins used the two-word name *shame-humiliation* for the affect is an indication that there are milder and more toxic extremes to the experience. Indeed, shame can range from very mild moments of embarrassment to deep feelings of humiliation even to the point of mortification. It is often the deepest negative moments of humiliation that cause people to batter and even kill one another or to take their own lives. In fact, FBI statistics for the decade from 1996–2005 show that more than 10% of law enforcement officers killed in the line of duty were responding to emergency calls about domestic violence. Being uninformed about shame is dangerous.

The Shame Family of Emotions

As mentioned earlier, while affects and feelings are inborn, emotions only develop over time. We are all different emotionally because the forces that act upon us as our nine innate affects progress into complex, adult emotions are unique to each individual. Different families, different cultures, different inborn temperaments, different sex hormones, and different genetic inheritance, among other things, all converge to influence our emotional development. It is beyond the scope of this book to go into detail about what makes us all appear so different emotionally; however, as will be discussed later, no matter how different we seem to be, if you really want to understand someone, learn the nine affects from which all of our personalities and emotions spring. Everyone knows and can share what it is like to feel shame, fear, distress, interest, enjoyment, surprise, anger, disgust, and dissmell. In this respect, we are much more alike than different from everyone else on earth, regardless of race, color, religion, or sexual orientation.

During the process of bonding with or attaching to parents, children become highly interested in their parents' approval. For small children (although one could argue the same is true for adults), the expression of parental approval takes place entirely through the showing of the positive feelings of interest and enjoyment. Therefore, disapproval of any kind triggers shame in a child because disapproval requires withdrawing positive affect from the relationship, even if temporarily. Since disapproval is mandatory if we are going to set proper limits for our children both to protect them from harm and to teach them how to be civilized adults, then the triggering of shame is necessary and appropriate in child-rearing. It is therefore inevitable as well as desirable that we learn to feel ashamed—an emotion only available to us because we evolved the inborn capacity to experience shame.

All members of the shame family of emotions emerge from the same intrinsic wiring in our brains, and all carry the same message or signal: *there is some type of blockage or impediment to our enjoyment or interest.* In spite of the fact that shame can only begin if something positive is going on first, it is a negative feeling and rapidly followed by what Nathanson called a "cognitive phase."[1] During this phase, we automatically search our memory—all the way back to childhood—to try to make sense out of what it is *about us* that would make us feel this way. (Because shame affect is present essentially from birth, the thoughts associated with it begin at an age when children are only capable of associating everything that happens with *themselves*—not because children are selfish, but because that is how immature brains function.)

From the earliest moments of feeling ashamed, triggered in the context of a child's normal relationship with his or her caregivers, an entire family of emotions related to shame gradually emerges. As our cognitive abilities advance with the maturing of our brains, and as we learn about ourselves by what our caregivers say and do, our response to shame begins to be associated with thoughts. Below I have paraphrased Nathanson's suggestions for the thoughts people often have during the cognitive phase of shame. These are highly unpleasant thoughts, but I am certain you will recognize having had one or more of them during shame experiences. (When I threw that golf club, I still clearly remember thinking at least numbers 1, 2, 3, 4, and 7, but 8 could have been there, too.) I list them here in eight general groups as follows:

1. I'm weak, incompetent, and stupid.
2. I'm completely helpless.
3. I'm a loser.
4. I'm defective.

---

1. Nathanson D.L. *Shame and Pride: Affect, Sex, and the Birth of the Self.* New York: Norton, 1992.

5. I'm ugly.
6. I'm sexually defective or unappealing.
7. I don't want anyone to see me right now. I need to disappear into a hole in the ground.
8. I'm unlovable and completely isolated from humanity.

Shame interacts with these thoughts in a circular way. Shame usually comes first and then the thoughts follow. However, any of these thoughts will trigger shame, creating a pattern of shame → shame thoughts → shame → shame thoughts and so on. When this pattern keeps repeating, a person can become stuck—like a computer frozen in a loop that will go on forever unless someone either turns it off or pushes the reset button. This is one of the reasons why at times things that have caused shame in us are very hard to forget, making the feeling linger much longer than we would like and imparting the sense that it is out of our control. This is also the reason shame is at the core of low self-esteem. You cannot have any one of that group of eight thoughts and feel good about yourself.

The combination of how shame is triggered and the thoughts that follow—thoughts uniquely related to each person's life experiences—leads to the variety of emotions found in the shame family of emotions. What follows is a very incomplete list of some of the members of that family, including a brief explanation of the dynamics:

Shame emotions from parent–child relationships. Children become highly interested in their parents' interest in them. Disapproval of the child by the parents occurs normally and is the impediment that triggers the earliest shame in children. This is the experience that leads to the normal appearance of the capacity that we all have to feel *ashamed*.

Shame emotions from relationships ending. If we are interested in a person and interested in that person being interested in us, then anything that blocks that interest will trigger shame. If that person leaves us or communicates they are no longer interested in us, our interest in being with them is blocked and we feel *abandoned* or *rejected*. There is a very strong connection between feeling ashamed and fears of abandonment.

Shame emotions from relationships floundering. When two people still have an interest in their relationship succeeding, if there is much discord (anger), this is an impediment that usually leads to *hurt* feelings; if there is more disconnection than discord, the impediment it creates leads to feelings of *distance* and *loneliness* even though the two people are still together.

Shame emotions from not wanting to be seen. Feeling *shy* has at its core the vulnerability—greater in some people than others—to experience shame. Very shy people avoid being seen because of their fear that others will see their imperfections—real or imagined. However, all of us, even those who are not shy, feel *exposed* when something that we were interested in keeping private is revealed to others. In this case, it is the revelation that acts as the impediment to interest.

Shame emotions from everyday impediments. If our interest in getting to an appointment on time is blocked by traffic, or our interest in opening one of those plastic-wrapped packages that totally resist almost all attempts is blocked by the demonic wrapping, or our interest in watching a TV show is blocked by the cable being down, or any one of a million other things like this happens, we feel *frustrated* or *disappointed*. (If the level of frustration or disappointment gets too great, we feel angry—a defense against shame that will be discussed in detail in Chapter 7.)

Shame emotions from more severe life impediments. If we have been fired from our job (an obvious trigger for shame), and our interest in finding a new job is impeded for a long time by an economic downturn, and our interest in supporting ourselves and our family is impeded by the lack of a job, we feel a sense of *helplessness* that over time can turn into *despair*. Or if we encounter an injury or illness that seems to be a permanent impediment to our interest in our former ability to perform physically, we will also feel helpless and perhaps despair.

Shame emotions from attacks on our character, race, religion, or political beliefs. If our interest and enjoyment in who we are and what we believe is impeded by the words, written or spoken, of others, we feel *discriminated* against and *disrespected*.

Shame emotions related to competition. I, like too many other Americans, grew up in a family that too often valued winning and being "number one" over the true spirit and fun of competition. Such families create too strong a connection between winning and the sense of one's personal value. This leads to a distorted interest in winning competitions rather than simply enjoying them for what they are. If one's interest in winning is too great, the impediment created by not winning can engender deep feelings of being a *weak, incompetent loser*.

Guilt is generally thought of as being distinctly different from shame. One sees written or hears the phrase "shame and guilt" as if they were completely separate phenomena. Guilt is, however, a special member of the shame family of emotions. We experience *guilt* when we have *shame* about something we have done, and then the *fear* of punishment for our bad deed, by either worldly or divine forces. In other words, guilt results from a combination of the two innate affects fear and shame. One difference that may help you understand the difference between shame and guilt is that shame is more about the self and turns us inward, while guilt is more what we have done to others and turns us outward.

I hope it is now clearer to you that shame, simply because of its natural function, is at the root of many emotions, most of which have nothing whatsoever to do with feeling *ashamed*. That premise is critical to understanding how relationships work and how learning to monitor shame in whatever disguise it assumes can be a vital tool in the successful maintenance of intimate relationships. The earliest roots of intimacy are the topic of the next chapter.

CHAPTER 3

Why People Want to Be Together

The core principle of affect psychology is that affects (or feelings) are the primary motivators of human behavior, including the desire to be in intimate relationships. I assure you that the affects are not mysterious things hidden deep in our unconscious; rather, they are simply a series of nine inborn reactions that provide us with information about the signals our senses receive. Because this function is so critical to the survival of our species, the affects have a very prominent role in the way our brains work. **One of the nine affects must be activated before we become aware of almost anything (pain being the major exception).** This means that one of the nine affects precedes and then accompanies every conscious experience in your life.

You might well object to that last sentence and say, "Wait just a minute. A lot of things go on in my life without me feeling anything at all!" I would not disagree that you are unaware at times of what you are feeling. Perhaps you might reconsider if I draw a parallel between affect and breathing. Most of the time, breathing occurs without awareness. We are used to breathing and do so automatically unless some toxin in the air or an illness in our lungs makes it difficult to breathe. Hold your breath for five seconds. Now you are aware of your breathing and will be aware for a few more seconds or minutes until it becomes automatic again.

Affects are triggered automatically, just like breathing. Affects are present from birth, just like breathing. We are usually unaware of the presence of affect because we have become used to it. I believe, for instance, that the most prevalent affect, one that is triggered many, many times every day, is *interest-excitement* (please see Appendix I for a complete description). We have interest in reading the newspaper or a book, interest in getting chores done (even if it is to relieve distress), interest in seeing our children or grandchildren, interest in our garden, interest in our significant other, interest in taking a walk or a drive, interest in watching a TV show, interest in listening to our favorite music, and interest in many, many other things every day. However, because we have done most if not all of these things before, the intensity of the interest is usually at a very low level. This lack of intensity makes it difficult to "feel" or be aware of the interest.

We do become aware if some factor intensifies interest. For instance, a dramatic happening in the world might trigger greater interest in the morning newspaper, or having been apart from our children or grandchildren will trigger great interest in their upcoming visit, just like having been confined to the house by horrible weather will trigger excitement when the sun finally comes out and we can take a walk or go running. In all of these situations, it is more obvious to us that we "feel" *interested* and are motivated by that interest to do something.

The general program in our brain that dictates the way the affects motivate us is a direct result of the fact that the positive affects of *interest* and *enjoyment* feel good, so we want to do more of what brings them on; and the negative affects of *fear, distress, anger, shame, disgust,* and *dissmell* feel bad and we want to either stop doing or avoid whatever causes them. This brain program for motivation—also called the **Central Blueprint**—mandates that we follow four basic rules from very early in life:

1. Positive feelings that make us feel good are to be maximally encouraged and fostered;
2. Negative feelings that make us feel bad are to be reduced to a minimum or eliminated;
3. Awareness of our feelings is to be encouraged so we can better carry out 1 and 2; and
4. We are to develop the power and skills necessary to do 1–3 to the fullest.

It is this underlying set of rules, preprogrammed in our brains from birth and operating like an internal computer program that never turns off, which leads us to want to be in relationships with other people. There have been many theories advanced over the years about why and how human infants become attached to those around them. I am not going to bore you with a review of those theories, the most popular of which is currently Bowlby and Ainsworth's "Attachment Theory." I am going to present you instead with a set of constructs based on affect script psychology and say simply about the other theories: they missed the boat because their originators lacked a clear, overarching theory of human motivation.

One more idea is worth mentioning before moving forward. Our brains specialize in pattern recognition for learning. The brain is very good at this. Learning takes place, in part, because the brain can compare patterns to one another and store them in memory. When an affect is associated with a pattern, it becomes important and meaningful in our lives. To fully understand emotional intimacy in adults, it will be useful to describe briefly the motivational sequence for the two most meaningful relationship patterns of early infancy. These two patterns are the starting point of all future relationships and are at the heart of why we really want to be together.

Relationship Pattern Number 1

While newborns can do a few special things such as distinguishing their own mother's breast milk from that of others, they have no attachment to anyone, including their birth mothers. Attachment to mother (or anyone who is the primary caregiver) first develops from a pattern that is repeated many, many times. This pattern appears for several reasons, two of which are of primary importance. The first is that the infant has the innate ability to experience the affect *distress-anguish* and thereby emit the cry of distress. The second is that affect is contagious—as anyone who has heard the piercing cry of distress from an infant sitting close to them on a crowded airplane will attest. Affect is also contagious visually. Just look at the picture of Katie, age ten months, signaling by her cry of distress that her new teeth hurt.

Does looking at the picture make you feel a little sorry for her? Did your face change expression and mirror hers? That feeling is mild distress in you.

Here is how affect and its contagious nature, directed by the Central Blueprint, create Relationship Pattern Number 1: Starting at birth, hunger, tiredness, wet diapers, or a number of other possible things can cause distress in the baby, and the innate affect distress-anguish is activated causing her to emit the cry of distress. Because distress is contagious, the baby's cry of distress triggers distress in the caregiver. The caregiver is motivated by his or her own distress (because of the need to follow rule number 2 and reduce negative affect) to find out and correct whatever is causing the infant's distress. Once fed or changed or rocked, the baby's distress is relieved. Relief of distress triggers contentment—the mildest form of the innate affect enjoyment-joy—in the infant, and the cry of distress stops. This in turn relieves distress in the caregiver and triggers enjoyment-joy in him or her.

Each day, the infant's experience of distress turning into contentment repeats many times over. As the infant's brain matures and she becomes more aware of the environment around her, she slowly begins to connect the relief of distress to the appearance of a person—and a pattern begins to form. At first, it matters little who the person is. But as an infant's perceptual abilities sharpen, she or he begins to prefer the primary caregiver more and more—the pattern, relief of distress, connects to a specific person. This association with or attachment to the caregiver is directed by the baby's Central Blueprint. Since she or he can now remember that this person makes them feel good when they had been feeling bad, following rule number 4, the baby develops the skills to help make it happen again. As a result, two seemingly opposite signs that an infant has attached to mother in this first relationship pattern are: 1) the baby in distress stops crying at the sight of mother and reaches for her, even before the cause of the distress has been relieved; and 2) a baby not in distress for any reason starts crying at the sight of mother and then stops as soon as she is picked up.

✦ First pattern that motivates us to want to be together: **When I feel bad, another person can make me feel good.**

It is well beyond the scope of this book to enumerate all the things that can go wrong in caregiver-infant relationships. However, a concept relevant to the appearance of shame problems in relationships is worth a brief mention. It has to do with situations where a caregiver, overloaded with fatigue or depression or work, either cannot respond consistently to her infant's distress or frequently responds with a negative affect such as anger. This alters the form of the initial attachment to the primary caregiver and unfortunate patterns develop. Rather than the positive pattern "when I feel bad, someone makes me feel good," negative patterns develop, such as "when I feel bad, nobody cares" or "when I feel bad, another person will make me feel worse by getting angry at me."

It is important to note, however, that even these negative patterns have their beginnings in the positive pattern of the initial attachment. All infants develop a very strong **interest** in this positive attachment pattern and an interest in maintaining it at any cost. Because impediment to interest triggers shame, many negative caregiver-infant interactions create shame in the infant. While it is difficult to know exactly how the infant experiences the various shame emotions, we do know that, as adults, people who have been exposed to negative caregiver-infant patterns can be prone to low self-esteem, rejection sensitivity, and even feelings of being isolated from the human race. The good news is that in spite of how much can go wrong, a great deal goes well enough in our earliest years that the majority of us do not want to be alone.

Relationship Pattern Number 2

While the first relationship pattern has its beginnings on day one of our lives, the second pattern does not start in earnest until the baby can smile. It usually takes between six and eight weeks before an infant's maturing brain and motor development permit the full smile of the affect *enjoyment-joy* to appear in all its glory. The contagious nature of those first smiles is so rewarding that everyone who experiences it tries their best to get the baby to smile again and again. When you look at this next picture of Katie, who is enjoying her applesauce and smiling at her grandmother, it more than likely will trigger at least a small smile in you.

Even your most straight-laced old uncle George will make the weirdest funny faces he can to get a baby to smile at him. Central Blueprint rule number 1 motivates Uncle George and the rest of us. The smile triggers so much positive feeling (enjoyment-joy) in us that we all develop a strong interest in repeating the experience. The baby does, too. It is this set of feelings that causes the baby and those around her to be interested in playing peek-a-boo, a game where the reappearance of the hidden face triggers enjoyment-joy time and time again. The pattern the baby learns from these interactions is that interest leads to enjoyment leads to more interest leads to more enjoyment and so on. This pattern becomes the second of the most basic motivators of why people want to be with other people.

✦ Second pattern that motivates us to want to be together: **People are interested in and enjoy me, and that makes me feel good and want to be interested in and enjoy them.**

I have stated these two basic relationship patterns somewhat simplistically. My patients taught me to do this. Over the years I have seen couples lose themselves in endless arguments fueled by the most complex rationalizations, defensive maneuvers, verbal and emotional manipulations, and confounding intellectualizations (aka BS) to prove who is "right." It often becomes necessary in the midst of all the emotional pain of such useless and usually repetitive disagreements to help them simplify things by shifting their focus. Therefore, I interrupt the argument—I can be louder than they at the drop of a hat—and ask them to reexamine their most basic, indispensable needs from the relationship. I have never had disagreement with the two ideas presented in this chapter, at least not from those who are still in love and really desirous of restoring harmony to their relationship. They want the other to show *interest* in and *enjoy* them; and they want the other to be their ally, helping them feel better in times of *distress*.

A critical problem for all of us is that clear awareness of the needs connected to these two relationship patterns diminishes somewhat as we age. There are two compelling reasons why this happens. The first has to do with "socialization." There is never any doubt about what our young children feel or need from us. We can see the affect written all over their faces. They do not disguise their excitement or their distress, or any of their other feelings, for that matter. However, the demands of parents, of teachers, and of society in general place tremendous pressure on children to reduce the intensity with which they express their feelings. We have all been shamed or made afraid of being too boisterous if we are excited about something or too whiny if we are in distress about something or too loud if we are angry about something. The demands of society and parents that children learn to minimize the expression of feelings and act more like "grownups" are necessary, but they come with a price. When we minimize the expression of our feelings, we become less aware of and less in touch with them. The more we do not know or are unaware of what we feel, the more difficult it is to communicate our needs, especially the most vulnerable ones, to our significant other.

The second reason we lose touch with our primary needs and feelings has to do with normal developmental issues related to healthy individuation. The process of interacting with the world and learning to be on our own requires that we be "self-sufficient" or "independent." We need to be able to take care of ourselves, to be interested in ourselves, to be able to relieve our own distress or other bad feelings without always having to count on others for help. We can and should feel proud when we accomplish this. And relationships between two people who can be self-sufficient and function independently, are generally happier and better equipped to deal with difficult problems. However, the price we pay for healthy individuation is that we must make ourselves less vulnerable—or at least appear and act that way to the outside world. The more we act not vulnerable, the more we lose track of our more vulnerable feelings and have difficulty sharing them with others. I will have much more to say about this later on, including some ideas about how to reverse this process. I only want to add here that this loss of familiarity with our feelings diminishes the awareness of self in many people, rendering them less able to manage the complex emotions created by normal relationship issues and helpless at handling the painful emotions of dysfunctional relationships.

I have no intention here of writing about all the complications and distortions that can take place in emerging relationship patterns as we move on from early infancy. There are reams of written material about relationship complexity, much of which I agree with. This book, on the other hand, is about simplification, about understanding the most basic elements that motivate human interpersonal interactions. If I am successful and communicate clearly in these pages, you will be able to analyze the positions taken by the many relationship theoreticians and boil down their propositions, no matter how complex or erudite they seem, into the two basic patterns I have presented in this chapter. We want to be in relationships with others, from casual friendships to deep, meaningful love affairs, because early in life we developed immutable patterns based on our interest and enjoyment of others, our interest and enjoyment in others being interested in and enjoying *us*, and the enjoyment we experience when others help us make negative feelings go away.

While this is not a book specifically about love, I propose that love, too, has the same bottom line as expressed in that last sentence. I will leave the definitions and descriptions of love to the plethora of poets and writers whose literary skills dwarf mine. I would note, however, that I conceive of love as a phenomenon based on the multifaceted internal images or patterns people form from the stored experiences of every sight, sound, feeling, taste, touch, ambience, person, dream, book, TV show, etc., etc., etc., amassed during his or her lifetime. This is a massive amount of data. I am uncertain as to whether scientists have yet invented a computer with enough storage capacity to contain all that accumulates in just one person. All of this information, most of it unconscious, goes into creating a vague mental pattern of the person we end up falling in love with, long before we met them.

Because the amount of information in any one person is overwhelming and mostly inaccessible, it is impossible to predict or really "know" why we fall in love with one "special" person and not with the many others who seem so similar. Nonetheless, when THE person comes into our lives, the image or pattern activates very, very powerful interest-excitement and joy, and "we just know" we are in love. And the bottom line: Once in love, what we all want from our lover is that they consistently show an interest in us and allow us to be interested in them, and that they help relieve bad feelings whenever we have them.

CHAPTER 4

Emotional Connections & Disconnections

In the previous chapter, I presented a simplified sketch of how, during infancy, our innate affects and feelings set the stage for powerful, lifelong patterns that motivate people to want and need relationships with others. Because our affects, feelings, and emotions are constantly changing—whether we recognize it or not—the emotional atmosphere of our relationships is also in constant flux, a matter I will address shortly. The fact that we all have the same inborn affects, coupled with the contagious nature of affects, is good news, good news, and bad news. The first good news is that, if we wish, we can understand and empathize with each other at the most basic levels. We all, man, woman, and child, know what it is like to feel fear, joy, excitement, distress, anger, and shame. The second good news is that when one of us is feeling good, the other can bask in the interest and joy we feel radiating from our partner. The bad news is that when the other is feeling bad, we too will begin to experience her or his fear, distress, anger, or shame. The shorthand method I use to refer to the complex interplay of feelings in relationships—also called interaffectivity—is *emotional connection.*

Emotional connections between people occur at many levels of depth and intensity over differing periods of time. We can feel momentarily connected to a perfect stranger on the street, catching each other's eye and nodding our heads in agreement as we both smile with enjoyment at some spectacle taking place before us. And we can feel the enduring connection to a life partner or a child for whose safety we would give up our lives. In this chapter, I will focus on the dynamics of emotional connection in couples who have *chosen* to spend their lives together. I am inexperienced with couples in *arranged* marriages, having treated only one such couple.

When two people fall in love, the emotional connection between them is strong, powered by intense feelings of interest-excitement. (I often refer to this phase of a relationship as "falling in heat," since the interest-excitement is usually at the excitement end of the scale.) Because the primary trigger for interest-excitement is *novelty*, it is easy to understand why the excitement of new love is so great. Here are two people who experience mutual "chemistry" with one another and who are completely novel to each other. Their past histories (biographies) are unknown to each other and wonderful to share. Their bodies and sexuality are new. Their friends, families, daily activities, hopes, dreams, and desires are new. She is interested in him and interested in him being interested in her, while he is interested in her and interested in her being interested in him, and so on. In other words, they share multiple layers of interest in each other. Because feelings and emotions are contagious, each person's interest continually triggers more interest in the other. The reflected interest is like two mirrors placed opposite one another in such a manner that the images reflect onward to infinity. It is a wonderful time in a relationship.

Novelty, of course, does not last forever. Therefore, it is impossible for such a high level of interest to last forever. As time goes by, the interest in one another begins to wax and wane, sometimes during a single day. Because of the way our brains are wired, one of the results of the diminishing of intense emotional interest is the triggering of feelings of enjoyment-joy (or contentment). Perhaps the most obvious example of this phenomenon occurs when intense sexual excitement ending in orgasm leads to contentment. For the couple newly in love, even if they chose to delay their sexual relationship, the alternation of moments of excitement with moments of the joy of being together is natural and easy.

New love also provides people with another source of enjoyment-joy. To feel that someone truly, deeply, wonderfully loves us relieves, at least for the moment, any distress, fear, or shame that we might be unlovable and would never find a suitable partner. Furthermore, it relieves the shame we may feel as we watch other people pair up and seemingly walk arm and arm into the sunset or dance merrily through the park while we sit alone feeling the pain of loneliness. Falling in love, therefore, is both a result of (is motivated by) and parallels the two patterns established early in childhood: when I feel bad, another person can make me feel good; and someone is interested in and enjoys me and that makes me feel good and I want to be interested in and enjoy them.

New love is also an atmosphere in which people can initially achieve their most intense levels of emotional intimacy. In 1996, in an academically oriented volume edited by Don Nathanson, *Knowing Feeling*, I presented the first affect script psychology–based definition of emotional intimacy in a chapter entitled "Affect and the Redefinition of Intimacy":

> Intimacy is an interaffective process through which the inmost parts of the self are communicated to the other by tangible displays of affect. These displays can take the form of verbal or nonverbal communication. They can involve touch, smell, hearing, facial expression, body language, sex, or cognition as when one shares with another some piece of information, a poem, a book, or a movie. The affect in an intimate relationship is triggered by stimuli generated in the here-and-now interactions between the two people, the scripts (patterns) formed in the childhood of both, and a complex interaction between these past and present phenomena.

The details of how I arrived at this definition are outside the scope of this book. (Please refer to *Knowing Feeling* if you have an interest.) But take note that for the remainder of this book, when I use the term *emotional connection*, I am referring almost exclusively to the kind of emotional intimacy defined above—a deep, intense level of emotional connection sought by two people who have fallen in love and who are desirous of spending the rest of their lives together, regardless of whether or not they have been married in an officially sanctioned civil or religious ceremony.

Because the affect system is the single most powerful force behind emotional connection, the Central Blueprint rules for motivation that direct us as individuals also direct us as couples. These rules are the essential ingredients for the healthy practice of the art of intimacy. Here is how I apply them to couples:

A healthy emotional connection is possible when two people

1. work together to create positive feelings as much as possible;
2. work together to do everything possible to reduce or eliminate negative feelings;
3. avoid hiding feelings from the other in order to better carry out 1 and

2; and

4. share in developing the power and skills necessary to do 1–3 to the fullest.

When a couple is able to develop patterns that allow them to follow these four rules in a balanced fashion, their relationship will have both the flexibility and strength to weather life's trickier, more difficult moments (or, as Shakespeare put it in Hamlet's famous soliloquy: "the slings and arrows of outrageous fortune"). They will be able to monitor their emotional connection in order to nurture it, massage it, and keep it alive and well. In other words, they will feel good about one another, feel close to one another, feel that the other has their back, feel warm and fuzzy about one another (both mentally and physically), feel the interest of the other coming their way, and enjoy the relationship.

If, after "falling in heat," two people stay together, the natural progression through time and getting to know one another reduces the novelty available for their interactions. Less novelty means there is less "we don't have to think about it, it just happens" interest-excitement in being together. Another way of stating this is that if a relationship is successful, people will almost inevitably begin to take one another for granted. I know many people who interpret this diminution in the intensity of their first blush excitement to mean that they are no longer in love.

For instance, while he was in high school, I began working with a young man who eventually married a woman he met in college. They had a very positive, comfortable, and sexually active relationship during their college years. They felt so strongly about one another that they were even able to overcome the dismay their parents expressed at their differing religious backgrounds, and they were married. As they both plunged into post-college education and careers, he began to experience a lack of sexual interest in her. This troubled him deeply because it did not appear to him that she had changed in any negative way. If anything, her body should have been more appealing because she had started working out regularly and dropped a few unneeded pounds. Of course, they also began to have more "disagreements" about the little things in their life—a fact that I am sure surprises no one who has been in a relationship longer than a couple of days, let alone a couple of years.

While both expressed some disappointment about the reduction in the frequency of their sexual interactions, it did not come close to being the major battle about sex that occurs in some marriages. This was because they both experienced a reduction in sexual interest in the other. This fact reduced the amount of shame about sex for this couple—the opposite of what one finds if one of the partners remains highly interested in sex and the other is not. Their disagreements tended to be mild and centered on the usual things couples fight about—money, in-laws, where to put the new sofa, etc. Overall, they got along moderately well and did not engage in angry, venomous exchanges.

Their emotional connection varied between a neutral state and a mildly negative state. Eventually, he had an affair. He felt so guilty about it that he confessed to her and they began marriage counseling (with someone not trained in the nuances of shame affect, its causes and effects). The counseling was not helpful. All it seemed to do was increase blame. They separated within a couple of years because their careers dictated moves to different cities, a separation that was welcomed by both. They agreed to date other people, but neither seemed interested in actively pursuing a formal divorce. They remained in contact over the next two or three years, seeing each other from time to time in what one might describe as a dating relationship. The frequency of their dates gradually increased and slowly their interest in one another grew stronger. They began to feel reconnected emotionally, a connection pleasant enough for them to resume sexual relations. The end of the story—at least as of this writing—is that they fell in love again, renewed their marriage vows, and she is pregnant with their first child.

While the path taken by this couple is somewhat unusual, what happened to their feelings for one another is not at all unusual. It is the normal, completely natural progression in **all** relationships that the intensity of the initial interest-excitement subsides, altering the very positive nature of the initial emotional connection. This couple mistook the "falling out of heat" for "falling out of love." As has been the case for many of us, because this was the first serious long-term relationship for both of them, they were young and naïve and mistook "falling in heat" for "falling in love."

Even though I have already declared that this is not a book wherein I will define love, I will share with you two opinions I have formed working with couples (including my own marriage) of all kinds—gay, lesbian, and heterosexual—since the late 1960s.

The first is that it takes about seven to nine years of living together for two people to experience enough of the good, the bad, and the ugly about self and other, of being confronted by the myriad of positive and negative situations that that amount of time forces upon every relationship, before the appearance of the certain knowledge that nothing will ever make them want to part. It is that knowledge, deep in one's heart and soul, which signifies the presence of adult, mature love. (I believe this is the origin of the sentiment expressed in the 1950s stage play, then movie, *The Seven Year Itch.* In the script, a married man remains in the city for the summer while his wife of seven years goes to the country with their son. He meets a beautiful, voluptuous woman who lives in the same apartment building. His sexual fantasies about her are vivid, but eventually lead him to the certainty that he will not have an affair because of what he feels for his wife.) Do not get me wrong; I know the powerful feelings of what I call "falling in heat" are real. They are wonderfully positive and exciting, and without them at the start, very few people would want to commit to a long-term relationship. But those feelings must pass. In mature love, there are negative moments, but the feeling of love does not pass.

The second thought on love is that there is not one person alive who can make anybody love anybody else. Only the two people involved have that power, even if they are not, like the rest of us, able to access all the information about the origin of those feelings. I did not fully understand this when I first began working with troubled couples in psychotherapy. I experienced shame at being ineffective when people did not fall back in love, even when I thought I was doing good work. It was partly this shame reaction that motivated me—with the help of others—to learn more about affect psychology and the roots of human motivation. (Ironically, it was only after learning about shame that I even knew that it was shame that motivated me to study about shame.) What I am now very certain of is that professional counselors, and the couples who seek their help, need to be clear that therapy cannot create love out of thin air. If it is gone, it is usually gone for good. But if the therapist and the couple repair an unhealthy emotional connection by removing the impediments that cause shame, love that has been repressed, suppressed, or otherwise hidden away can be rekindled.

As I return to the main topic of this chapter, I must confess that I do not have an exact definition of *emotional connection.* I know it when I feel it, and I suspect that you also know it when you feel it. It is very clear that when we talk about positive things and look into each other's eyes, we are emotionally connected. We feel "close." But we can and usually do feel emotionally connected when we sit together and watch a movie or share a bottle of wine or go for a drive or take a walk or have great sex or see eye to eye politically or have a great debate about our political differences or watch our kids playing or just sit together quietly in the same room. These are all situations where the blueprint motivating the emotional connection leads us to share and foster positive feelings (rule number 1).

The discussion and resolution of a difficult matter about which we each felt distress would be an example of the blueprint promoting emotional connection by leading us to share and help diminish negative feelings (rule number 2). While it is difficult to feel connected when we have negative feelings, the sharing and resolution of them definitely provides relief and triggers feelings that are more positive. If someone is either unaware of or will not share their feelings, even though we can read their feelings to some extent by watching their face and other body language, then rule number 3 will be violated. This creates an emotional atmosphere wherein it is more difficult to follow the first two rules. Simply stated, emotional connection is almost impossible with someone who withholds their emotions.

The bottom line about emotional connection is that it is present when we feel our partner's interest-excitement in us and our partner feels our interest-excitement in return; and it is present when we feel the enjoyment-joy (contentment) from something our partner does to relieve bad feelings (fear, distress, or shame) in us or when we do the same for him or her. In other words, emotional connection follows the very first relational patterns we developed in early childhood.

The normal daily activities of two people in a relationship prevent them from feeling emotionally connected at all times. We are less likely to feel emotionally connected when we are not together, especially if we are experiencing strong emotions from something else, like an emergency at work. However, even when apart, we can imagine our significant other and feel connected by our positive thoughts about them. Being apart, of course, is a simple reality that we accept as long as we understand and have mutually agreed upon the reasons for it. One of the wonderful things about vacations together is that we do not have to be apart or focus on earning a living or running a household or pleasing a boss or doing chores or any of the things that require separate, individual attention. Furthermore, vacations provide us with novel settings away from our everyday lives, and novelty increases the general level of interest-excitement in both of us, providing wonderful fuel for the fire of our emotional connection.

Emotional disconnection occurs when one partner does not understand or agree with the reasons for the absence of the other, or when the two are in the same physical space but there is no sharing of interest or enjoyment—"he's here but he's not really here." The presence of unresolved conflicts that hover beneath the surface, the absence of physical touch, the inability of one, the other, or both partners to either be aware of or speak about their feelings, and the presence in one, the other, or both of strong negative feelings of distress, fear, anger, shame, or disgust are just a few of the things that lead to a sense of emotional disconnection.

The bottom line about emotional disconnection is that it is caused by *impediments* to our interest or enjoyment of one another, a disruption in the childhood patterns of interpersonal attachment. And this brings us back to the hidden challenge of shame.

As bad as shame feels, it would be an interpersonal tragedy if it were not present to signal us that something has blocked our emotional connection and taken away the good feelings.

The healthy practice of the art of intimacy requires that we learn about shame and accept it for what it is: a message that an impediment is destroying our emotional connection. In the chapters that follow, I encourage you to find shame wherever it is hidden in order to learn how to accept the challenge it presents.

CHAPTER 5

Impediments, Impediments, Impediments

Including "A Primer of Affect Psychology" in Appendix I and the title of this chapter, I have used the word *impediment* more than thirty times in this book. Having decided it was about time to make clear what I mean when I use that word, I consulted an online thesaurus, which produced a list with more than fifty synonyms. Instead of overloading you with that list, I thought it best to simply describe its role in affect psychology and then present a series of vignettes as examples of how and when impediments to emotional connection occur.

The innate affect *shame* evolved because the positive affects of *interest-excitement* and *enjoyment-joy* were so rewarding, so pleasant, and so desirable that our earliest ancestors wanted to feel them often and for as long as possible. In order to keep an eye, as it were, on these positive feelings, our forbearers needed something that would give a clear message, a signal of some kind, whenever good feelings stopped before they were ready for them to stop. There was no need for a signal in situations where the interest-excitement or enjoyment-joy had simply come to a natural end, where whatever had produced the good feelings simply lost its charm. No; this signal was only important if, while still in the middle of feeling good and wanting it to continue, **something** got in the way. That **something** is what I mean by an **impediment**. It, as you will learn in this chapter, can be any one of a million things.

When that **something** blocks, obstructs, hinders, or just plain gets in the way of our good feelings, a bad feeling—*shame-humiliation*—is triggered, and immediately our attention is directed to the impediment.

This provides an opportunity, if we have the necessary tools, for removal of the impediment and a return of the good feelings. (Of course, it would not have made sense—or satisfied the evolutionary need—if the signal that evolved had also been a good feeling, because that would only divert attention from the current object of our interest or enjoyment rather than let us know something had gotten in the way. That kind of diversion is what frequently happens to people with ADHD and makes it difficult for them to remain focused on the real objects of their interest. Imagine a human race with no ability to maintain focus on or pursue things that seem interesting. We would be a mess and incapable of maintaining attention long enough to invent even the simplest of things. Hence shame-humiliation, as we are all too aware, feels bad.)

You and I have experienced the affect or feeling of *interest* so frequently in our lives—literally thousands of times each day—that most of the time when it occurs, it is not very intense, and we are usually not even aware of it. This fact has made interest, possibly the most frequently occurring of all the feelings, the least studied by researchers in the field of human emotion. They only seem to take notice of interest when something goes very right with it and it becomes excitement or when something goes very wrong with it and it is completely lost, as in depression—and even then researchers tend to focus not on the loss of interest but on the negative factor causing the depression.

It is great fun, and of great interest, to observe interest in children. To them, almost everything is new. As a result, their interest is more intense—often approaching excitement—and therefore more apparent. I recently observed my one-year-old twin granddaughters tearing through my house, looking at everything, touching everything they could reach, often squealing in excitement at some new item, and discovering the only non-childproof cabinet in my bathroom—the one containing the poisons, of course. When I—as impediment—picked them up and moved them away, they had a brief moment of frustration (very mild shame) and returned immediately to the cabinet. It took some of their mother's old stuffed animals to capture their interest in another room and divert them from picking up poison containers, which I then secured behind a locked bathroom door. While it is much easier to observe how often *interest-excitement* is triggered in children, and obviously there is less novelty in adult life, this does not mean that adults do not have interest (and/or excitement) triggered frequently. Most of the time, however, adult interest is simply less intense, more mild interest than excitement, and hence less noticeable.

One summer when my eldest daughter was young, my interest turned to butterflies. I had given her a butterfly collecting kit for Christmas, hoping she would develop an interest and it would become something we could enjoy doing together. We studied the pictures in the book that came with the kit and caught a few interesting butterflies the next spring, but mostly we had a lot of fun scanning the fields and woods searching for new species to capture. Today this would be called father-daughter bonding.

Early in the summer of that same year, I went with a friend to play tennis on the courts of his school, courts located next to a large field that remained uncut when school was not in session. As we entered the courts, I looked over at the field and saw what must have been nearly 5,000 small white cabbage butterflies (wingspan about two inches) fluttering above the tall grass. I was amazed and said to my friend, "Wow, look at all those butterflies!"

He looked at the field and said, "I don't see any butterflies." When I directed his attention to an area about a foot above the uncut grass, he suddenly saw all the butterflies and startled. Later than night, we were dining with our wives on his deck when a beautiful monarch butterfly floated past on the breeze. He remarked, "You've changed the way I look at butterflies."

My goal for this book, although I do not expect it to happen as dramatically as it did that day for my friend, is to stimulate your interest so that you change the way you look at and monitor your emotional connection with your significant other. The motivating force for that connection is affect, especially the positive affects of interest-excitement and enjoyment-joy, which are, happily, as ubiquitous as butterflies, but, unhappily, can be impeded by many things. This means that moments of shame are also as ubiquitous as the butterflies in the field.

The very best way to monitor any emotional connection is by being aware of how it makes you feel, with extra-special attention paid to the first few moments it begins to feel bad. When some impediment to emotional connection occurs—and it does not matter at all if the impediment is intentional or unintentional, by one partner or the other, or by something completely outside your control as a couple—shame affect is triggered. As previously mentioned, the nine innate affects, including shame, are just part of our *biology*, and much like the knee-jerk reaction, we have no control over them. It is simply part of our natural wiring to have shame affect set off if our ongoing interest in an emotional connection to someone is blocked, impeded, hindered, or otherwise withheld from us.

It is vitally important to remember that when one experiences the affect shame, it is much more than simply feeling **ashamed.** The reaction might also include one or more of the shame family of emotions outlined in Chapter 2. Because our backgrounds (our biographies) are so varied, our emotional experience of shame can vary greatly, too. Generally, however, the emotions most commonly experienced when the affect shame-humiliation is triggered in interpersonal relationships include feelings of **rejection, isolation, hurt,** and/or a sense of *feeling distant* from the other. These are the **signals** you need to be looking for to monitor impediments to emotional connection.

Hopefully, the frequency with which impediments occur in your relationship is not that great, but it will not (nor can it ever be) zero. On a technical note: When the intensity level of the impeded interest-excitement or enjoyment-joy is high, the shame emotions triggered, the rejection or hurt, are much more intense; and when the positive emotions impeded are mild before being blocked, the shame is also mild. (After all, there are very large butterflies—the largest being the Queen Alexandra's Birdwing in Papua New Guinea with a wingspan up to a foot—and very small butterflies—the smallest having been discovered in Shaanxi Province, China, in 2002, with a wingspan as small as 12 mm, or about half an inch.)

One patient of mine had her boyfriend and fiancé of eight years break up with her rather suddenly. Her interest in the relationship was, of course, very intense and included visions of marriage, children, and growing old together. Not surprisingly, the shame triggered in her was at the level of intensity known as humiliation. It produced very strong emotions of hurt, rejection, and loss that she could not get out of her mind. Lying awake at night, she would go over and over all the things she imagined she had done wrong that made him leave her. These painful ruminations rendered her unable to sleep more than two or three hours at a time for months. On the other side of the spectrum was the patient who was dating someone in whom she was only mildly interested for a couple of months. When he decided to end the relationship, she had a mild shame reaction; felt momentarily rejected, and then decided she was probably better off, as she had no real interest in the relationship becoming a long-term affair. She slept poorly for only one night.

Once you begin to monitor your emotional connection more closely, you will have mastered the first step in the art of using shame to enhance intimacy. Almost everyone in a relationship is doing something to try to achieve that already, even though very few know it is shame that is helping them. The second step is to locate the impediment to emotional connection that is triggering the shame. In the chapters that follow, I intend to give you a number of ideas to help with what I call "impediment removal," because learning rapid and efficient restoration of the positive feelings that make emotional connection rewarding can save relationships. Before doing so, however, I want to provide you with several other pieces of information about shame, including how overly intense shame—whether brought to the relationship from childhood issues or a direct result of something very negative in the couple's interaction—leads to defensive reactions that prevent us from recognizing shame. Those defenses can lead couples into what I call "Compass of Shame spirals" that devastate and ruin relationships.

But first, here are a few examples of everyday and not-so-everyday impediments to emotional connection that trigger shame. As you review these examples, keep in mind that it does not matter whether the impediment is the result of a brief event lasting only a few seconds or minutes, or the result of something that takes place over a long period of time. Shame is triggered either way.

Impediment from communication failures. No book about relationships can avoid discussing problems in communication. This book is no different, but the emphasis here is not on the actual words but on whether the communication maintains or impedes emotional connection. For instance, two people can sit together without speaking and remain emotionally connected because they are engaged in some form of nonverbal communication that promotes positive feelings of interest and enjoyment. Examples of this include holding hands walking in the woods, snuggling on the couch watching a TV show, sitting side by side on deck chairs gazing at the sun setting over the Pacific while vacationing in Mexico, or taking a drive together to see the fall foliage in the Berkshires.

There are, of course, many other times when not talking to one's partner is a major impediment. If one does not expose one's feelings to the other, then the other finds her interest blocked. If one does not inquire about the other, then the other finds her interest in him being interested in her blocked. That this is so is obvious; what is less obvious is that the **normal response to blocked interest is to feel shame**. So if you have a partner who does not talk to you and you feel rejected or hurt by that behavior, what you are feeling is 100% normal; don't let anyone ever convince you otherwise.

However, there are many verbal communications that trigger shame directly and thereby impede emotional connection. Examples of this include speaking in a negative tone of voice, blabbing on with no regard to what one's partner feels, using judgmental words like *lazy* or *stupid* when referring to one's partner, as well as any other form of verbal put-down. Using certain clichés when talking to your partner, especially "you're just like a man" or "you're just like a woman," is shaming because it trivializes the other's existence, does not recognize the individual being spoken to, and does not communicate what you are really feeling. (The ability to expose clearly one's innermost feelings to the other is absolutely critical for the maintenance of healthy, happy, and rewarding emotional connections—more about this in later chapters.)

Hearing loss can be another communication impediment that makes emotional connection difficult. The inability to hear the emotions communicated by the tonal inflections in the speech of another is an impediment because it prevents one from feeling what the other is feeling, whether those feelings are positive or negative. Infants respond positively to the positive affect in a caregiver's voice, even if it comes from another room. And, of course, if the other cannot hear us and often does not respond to our words, that, too, is an impediment.

Impediment from affect mismatch. This is one of the most common causes of impediment. It happens when what one person is feeling is of much greater intensity, completely different, or totally unrelated to what their partner is feeling. For instance, you come home greatly excited about a recent experience, only to find your partner deeply engrossed in a TV show. When you start to tell her about your experience, she shushes you and turns back to the TV. Obviously, this means you need to wait until the show is over to talk about your good time. However, there is a moment of feeling rejected—mild shame—when her *shush* impedes your desire (your interest) to connect with her and share your excitement.

The ritual of two people sitting down together with a drink or a glass of wine at the end of the workday evolved to help remove such impediments. Knowing that they have set aside a time to reconnect—whether it includes alcohol or not—protects both members of the couple from experiencing rejection when the other is not immediately "tuned in" to them. A kiss at the door, no matter if it is perfunctory, helps also. When used properly, alcohol can relieve the distress of the daily grind, making it easier to focus on and connect emotionally to each other. On the other hand, if one person is already feeling "mellow" from the effects of a drink or two taken before meeting up with their partner, and the partner has not had a drink, shame is likely to be triggered by an affect mismatch created by the booze.

"That's just the booze listening."

[*The New Yorker*, October, 5, 2009, pg 33.]

In the cartoon, she looks angry because she has had shame triggered by the impediment of his being "too mellow" and not tuned in to her emotions. Her anger is a defense against shame known as *attack other*, a defense discussed in detail in the next chapter. A greater problem arises from the excessive use of alcohol. Excessive use creates biochemical changes in normal brain functioning and a general withdrawal into the self, often in ways that act as impenetrable impediments. As a result, there can be little or no emotional connection with a chronic alcoholic who continues to drink.

Before my wife retired from teaching first grade, she often commented that it was a good thing she left the house in the morning before I woke up. She was right. I have never been a good sleeper; too many things seem to disrupt my sleep too easily, and I have a biological clock that is the opposite of hers. Her day/night clock is set on early to bed, early to rise, and she loves to talk in the morning. My clock is set on late to bed, and I don't believe I have to get up so darn early, and I'm still too tired and too sleepy to want to talk in the morning. This affect mismatch between us triggered shame in her, even though I insisted it was me and not her that was the cause of the problem (the impediment). She really enjoyed leaving the house early to teach. It meant she did not have to be subjected to my grumpiness (distress), and she could talk to her great friends Sue and Wendy to her heart's content.

You can probably recall many such situations in which the affects of you and your partner were miles apart. This does not always act as an impediment, but it frequently does. During those moments when it does, we do not feel connected. This is not always a problem because couples generally understand that they cannot be emotionally connected 24/7. It is, however, always a problem if one partner is in distress and the other is not emotionally available to help relieve that distress. Then the feelings of shame and rejection can lead to serious problems.

Impediment in long-distance relationships. I have worked with more than a few couples who had serious relational problems because they lived in different cities or their work caused them to be apart for long periods of time. Emotional connection requires a steady sharing of feelings. We cannot know for certain that the other is really interested in us unless we "feel" it. The best way to "feel the feelings" of another—to be emotionally connected—is to be in their presence so that we can see their facial expressions and body language, and be able to touch and be touched by them. Telephone conversations only convey part of that information through the words spoken and tone of voice used. New technologies like Skype are exciting in that we can see the face of the other person as they talk, but there is still an impediment to touch. So when we hang up the phone or disconnect from a computer link, there is an inevitable impediment to our emotional connection. The shame that is triggered can lead to feelings of loneliness that, in worst-case scenarios, can begin to make us feel alone, isolated, and unlovable, especially if the conversation did not go well.

I remember only too well experiencing such feelings my freshman year in college. I had fallen in love—my first time—with a girl when we were both juniors in high school. As young lovers do, over the next two years we made many plans about our future together. After we graduated from high school, we went to colleges separated by over 400 miles. Neither of us had the use of a car, and no one had even heard of such a thing as a cell phone or a computer or the Internet at that time. Once each week, I would gather up all my loose change, head over to the student union, and wait for a pay phone to become available—that's right, this was even before students were allowed telephones in their dorm rooms. I was so excited before each call, I could hardly wait. But when the call did not live up to my expectations—because there is no way it could equal the feeling of what it was like being together—I would begin to feel something very negative that I now know is shame. I usually felt lonelier after the call than I did before.

The changes that took place in each of us during the long months apart, combined with the inability to spend much time feeling emotionally connected, eventually led to the end of the relationship. This is a very common result when two people attempt a long-term/long-distance relationship. Long distances and long periods of time apart are impediments to emotional connection. This triggers shame, then loneliness, and many times jealousy (see the next chapter). These feelings rob a relationship of its positive affect, reducing the motivation of the partners to remain together.

Impediment from physical illness. Conditions that impair our sense of well-being, like the flu or a very bad cold or pneumonia, severe chronic pain, or a myriad of other things, create strong negative feelings, especially distress-anguish, in the sick person. Such strong feelings impede emotional connection because the sick person naturally withdraws into the self in what I believe is a normal survival mechanism. We have all had the experience of being sick with the flu, every joint in our body aching, head throbbing, feeling weak as a kitten, and reduced to worrying whether we are going to die but not really caring because then maybe we would feel better. When we are so sick, the illness robs us of our energy and our ability to be interested in anything. In the case of the flu, our partner easily recognizes the condition and can accept the temporary impediment to emotional connection without feeling shame, especially when he shifts his interest in emotional connection to nursing his loved one back to health.

The situation is more problematic when the partner has a long-term chronic illness such as lupus or rheumatoid arthritis or any other serious condition that lasts for many years. Such illnesses can render a person too sick, too distressed, and in too much pain to have much if any interest in their partner. This places even the most understanding of partners in a position of blocked emotional connection for months or years at a time. If that partner protects herself from feeling lonely, isolated, and rejected by removing interest in the other, then a compromised relationship will exist. And yet, that is her only real defense against shame in this situation. Most people who are comfortable staying in such relationships are able to do so because they shift their interest and make good connections with other people or with their church groups or other organized activities.

So-called mental illnesses belong in this section on physical illness also. The more researchers discover about the brain, the clearer it is that illnesses like schizophrenia, bipolar disorder, depressive disorders, many anxiety disorders, and attention deficit hyperactivity disorder (ADHD), just to mention a few, are caused by biological glitches in the brain. The diseased biology produces the psychological symptoms, not the other way around. The psychological symptoms act as serious impediments and can last many months or years. These issues are discussed in greater detail in Chapter 12.

Impediment from lack of awareness of self. The childhood experiences of many people engender in them a lack of awareness of their own feelings. This happens, for instance, in families with parents who are overloaded emotionally for some reason and unable to handle any negative emotion coming from their children. Their kids often learn that it is better/safer not to express any emotion, and by not doing so over long periods of time, they lose the ability to be in touch with their emotions. As adults, such people are often unable to know what they are feeling, and this leads to communication failures. After all, if I don't know what I'm feeling, how can I let *you* know what I'm feeling? Because the fuel for emotional connection is the sharing of feelings, the inability to know one's feelings acts as an impediment. Partners of those who are distant from their feelings often feel emotionally isolated in the relationship and can experience strong feelings of rejection, especially if the other is prone to long periods of silence.

Impediment from outside sources. An October 2010 issue of *Time* magazine carried a prediction that for the first time in history, the "workplace" will soon have a greater number of women than men. Over the past two decades, I have worked with a growing number of families where both members of the couple have careers. If they also have children, the time and energy required to manage both can act as an impediment to emotional connection. If they do not set aside time to spend together, they can drift very far apart emotionally, sometimes with little awareness that this is happening. Next thing they know, they begin to wonder if they are still in love.

Children, though we love them dearly, can be an impediment. They can get in the way of moments we have planned to spend together. A man once told me the story of an evening he and his wife had set aside to watch a movie at home. She had been feeling a little lonely (emotionally disconnected) because of their hectic schedules, even though they were retired, and just that day had shared those feelings with him. He understood and agreed with her. They made some joint plans for the coming weeks, including a driving trip to Mount Rushmore, but decided to start that very night by watching a movie together. Just the process of talking and making those decisions had already reestablished their positive feelings.

However, no sooner had they sat down together on the couch, than the phone rang. The call was from her son. (They each had a son from a prior marriage.) My friend told me that he had expected there to be a brief interruption because it was not unusual for her son to call, but seldom did his calls last for more than a few minutes. However, this phone conversation lasted over an hour. As time passed, he found himself feeling more and more rejected. It was as if there had been a warm, loving buildup to being close, but now she was in the other room and he was stuck on the couch alone. Fortunately, his understanding of affect psychology helped him remain aware of these feelings. As a result, he was able to keep the negative feelings in perspective and even laughed to himself when he caught a series of jealous thoughts running through his mind. One cannot stop such feelings in situations like this because we are wired to experience shame when impediments occur. He shared his thoughts and feelings with his wife when she finally got off the phone, and her immediate understanding of his feelings reestablished their emotional connection on the spot.

There is another common "impediment" situation related to children that could be called the "our empty nest was so quiet, but now it's too full" syndrome. Quite a few couples have shared with me that something strange happens to their relationship when the kids come home from college. These are couples who found themselves much better able to maintain their emotional connection after the kids grew up and moved out. Without all the hassles of child-rearing that can act as impediments, many couples rediscover their warm feelings toward one another, only to find it strange that when the kids reappear, they have a negative reaction either to one another or to the children. They feel the kids imposing themselves, whether intentionally or unintentionally, between the two of them.

I worked with a couple several years after their daughter, an only child, had gone away to college. This couple had used therapy well and felt quite hopeful about the future of their relationship. They had been very disconnected for many years—so much so that their daughter had learned she could easily play the two of them off against each other. After graduation, she returned home to live and immediately reinserted herself between them. I saw them several months later, and all of their therapeutic gains had been lost. They were at one another's throats again, uncertain whether they wanted to remain married. It took some more work in therapy for them to learn how to keep their grown child from being an impediment to their own emotional connection.

Impediment from intense emotion. If one's partner is experiencing a moment of extremely intense emotion, it is difficult to connect with her or him. As a part of my training in child psychiatry, I spent time on the cancer unit at Children's Hospital of Philadelphia. In the late 1960s and early 1970s, the treatment of childhood leukemia was relatively unsuccessful compared to today's standards. Some of the children with leukemia returned to the hospital time and time again on the brink of death, only to recover and go home once more. Eventually, however, far too many died from the disease. This process subjected the parents of these children to the repeated intense negative affects of fear-terror and distress-anguish. It was noted by the medical staff that there seemed to be a very high divorce rate in these families. (As far as I know, there was no research to prove this at the time.) I believe that the intensity of the negative emotions experienced by the parents of these children created serious impediments to their emotional connection, leading to frequent episodes of unmanageable shame and eventual dissolution of many marriages.

Impediment from sexual problems. Everyone has experienced shame related to sex at some time in their lives. Sexual issues can be very difficult impediments to overcome. In Chapter 11, I briefly explore this complex subject.

Intense anger, whether in one person or both, is always a powerful impediment to emotional connection, even when not directed at one's partner. You simply cannot get close to a person who is experiencing a moment of rage. (See Chapter 7 for a detailed look at the subject of anger and shame.)

Impediments to emotional connection can arise at any time and in many more situations than the ones outlined here. In order to use the information available from shame affect triggered by such impediments, one must first be aware of the shame. It might seem at first glance that this would be easy. In reality, it is very difficult. The unpleasant nature of shame compels everyone to build defenses against it. The most successful defenses are those that make us completely unaware of shame in both ourselves and others. The next chapter is about those defenses.

CHAPTER 6

A Compass & A Triangle

It is remarkable to me that during my psychiatric training from the late 1960s to the mid 1970s, I do not remember the word *shame* being mentioned by my mentors. If spoken, it was only in passing. No teacher or supervisor or lecturer ever formally addressed the psychology of human shame in depth. Fortunately, things have changed. For example, a recent search for "shame" on amazon.com produced a listing of over 300 books with that word in the title. Very few of these books were published before 1990, and only two or three of them were written by authors informed by affect psychology. (In Appendix II, there is list of books on various subjects by authors versed in affect psychology.)

The current trend recognizes the *importance of shame* when considering issues of discrimination, sexual abuse, alcoholism, dysfunctional families, religion, narcissism, guilt, gays, lesbians, apartheid, poverty, obesity, abortion, holocaust survivors, church and military cover-ups, among others. However, most people do not recognize the frequent presence of shame in their daily lives and relationships. The reasons for this have mostly to do with the fact that shame is an unpleasant feeling, so unpleasant that even saying the word is difficult for many people.

From early childhood on, we all develop defenses against shame in order to disguise or reduce its unpleasant nature. These defenses are, in part, why shame remains a hidden challenge to most relationships. This chapter is about those defenses and a couple of handy ways—in the forms of a compass and a triangle—to help you recognize shame in its many disguises. Knowing when shame is triggered in interactions between you and your loved ones is vital to this book's purpose. I want to equip you with the ability to use the information provided by shame to enhance the skills with which you practice the art of intimacy.

Before turning to a detailed discussion of shame defenses, it is worth listing briefly some of the other reasons that the innate affect shame-humiliation is difficult to recognize, not only for you but for researchers in human psychology as well. The items in this list include several of the reasons for the diminished awareness of all affect in all of us—a serious detriment for human interrelatedness to self and others because it is not "I think, therefore I am," but rather "I *feel*, therefore I am" that directs our awareness of who we really are.

1) As discussed in the first chapter, shame leads to an entire family of emotions that do not feel like being ashamed or embarrassed and therefore are not recognized as originating in shame.

2) The fact that shame is triggered by impediments to the positive affect interest-excitement has led researchers astray for many years because interest-excitement occurs in us so frequently from the moment of birth on, it becomes as invisible as the air we breathe. Most researchers in human emotion do not recognize interest as one of the basic, inborn roots of our emotions. As a result, interest and impediments to it are seldom the subject of neuropsychological research.

3) Chronic childhood shame, whether of biological or psychological origins, can influence the development of the whole personality in ways that make shame disappear. For instance, when people say someone has a "big ego," they are usually describing someone with a narcissistic personality. These are people who have so much shame they cannot tolerate anyone seeing weaknesses in them. They act as if they are above everyone else because they consciously believe that they are too smart or too expert at what they do to be wrong, ever. They are usually unpleasant people to be around and very difficult to relate to emotionally. It is as if their whole demeanor is a put-down to the rest of the human race. Their rigidity creates a wall around them that is essentially impenetrable by others, to the point that they have frequent and terrible marriages. Narcissistic people become so skilled at hiding their shame that neither they nor those around them can see it. I encourage you to look for shame whenever you hear someone referred to as having a big ego.

4) In general, all children are systematically shamed out of being aware of feelings during the process called socialization. Our culture has

unwritten demands that its citizens not make too much noise in public. Thus it is shameful to "cry like a baby" or exhibit raw displays of anger, or even to be too noisily excited about something. One often sees parents of young children doing their best to shush kids who are noisy.

"If you bring joy and enthusiasm to everything you do, people will think you're crazy."

[*The New Yorker*, May 9, 2011, pg 49.]

This demand that a person's affect be muted extends into schools, the workplace, and the community at large. Due to the contagious nature of affect, there are good reasons for minimizing the display of affect at its most intense. For instance, all of us are very uncomfortable when a nearby baby is crying in distress and we are in a confined space such as an airplane or elevator and cannot escape hearing the cries. The problem is that constant shaming reminders to a child to suppress feelings around others creates in the child a sense that something is very wrong with them, that they are inferior in some way. The easiest way to hide feelings is to suppress them so that they never appear at all. This process, which is found in many cultures, creates a serious lack of self-awareness. Our affects, feelings, and emotions are our most basic motivators. As I said earlier, if you do not know what motivates you to do things, how can you really understand who you are?

5) In most instances when shame is triggered, a defense to make us feel less uncomfortable is activated. By the time we become adults, these defenses are automatic and activated so rapidly after shame is triggered—possibly in nanoseconds—that shame does not register in awareness. Any shame defense that makes us unaware of the shame is a successful

defense to the extent that we remain truly unaware. However, defenses against shame have other consequences, many of which are damaging for us as individuals and for our relationships.

In extensive research for his book *Shame and Pride*—research that reached back as far as the 1500s—Don Nathanson discovered that defenses against shame could be placed into four general categories. Knowing the defensive patterns found in each of these four categories is essential if you are going to be able to decode behaviors that hide both *your* shame and that of your significant other.

✦ CRITICAL POINT: **It is very important to keep in mind that because these defenses are now second nature to you, you will have to work backwards to recognize that shame preceded the defense.**

In other words, you will need to say to yourself, "Oh, I only withdraw or attack [for example] after I've had a shame reaction." Once you have refined your awareness of your own shame and recognize its appearance when certain things happen between you and your partner, you will have decoded your own behavior in ways that will enhance your relationship.

The Compass of Shame

Nathanson decided to use the image of a compass because the two pairs of shame defenses are somewhat the opposites of one another. This also makes them easier to remember. As I describe each of the four groups, you will undoubtedly find some aspect of yourself in each. All of us have used every one of these defensive actions at one time or another, and sometimes all of them in the same day. These defensive maneuvers—except in their extreme forms—should not be considered either good or bad or the right or wrong way to do things. They are the result of a very natural human ability and a powerful need to reduce feelings of shame when we do not know what else to do with them. Each of us finds our most comfortable pattern of defense and uses that pattern as our go-to response as soon as shame is triggered.

The set of defenses any one of us settles upon are learned from inter-actions with and observations of those in our childhood environment. They become "unconscious" responses so that we do not have to think about them; that is, they occur automatically when we experience shame. My ultimate goal here is to help make you "conscious" of the shame that precedes each defensive reaction to that unpleasant emotion. Only then will you to be able to use the information provided by shame to alert you to the presence of impediments to your emotional connection, things that prevent you from feeling close to one another. Otherwise, shame does more harm than good.

Here is my rendition of the image of the Compass of Shame:

WITHDRAWAL

ATTACK OTHER  ATTACK SELF

AVOIDANCE

Attack Other Defenses

"I'm OK but you're not!"

This group of shame defenses works by shifting attention away from the self and onto another person or thing. Anger is almost always involved because angry feelings make more vulnerable feelings like shame disappear. However, for many individuals anger is also taboo, and they hide it behind such things as passive-aggressive behaviors. Nonetheless, when we are good and angry, we pump some adrenaline, grit our teeth, clench our fists, stomp our feet, throw things, and generally feel more powerful. Why do we do this? Because shame makes us feel defective, weak, helpless, ugly, stupid, and like disappearing into a hole in the ground, while anger, on the other hand, makes us feel strong so that the weaker feelings disappear—at least temporarily. However, as Freud and others have taught us, not all anger is the foot-stomping kind; some, like sarcasm, is more subtle.

Here is a partial list of behaviors, each with a representative quote or thought, exhibited when shame is covered up by the use of *attack other* methods of defense:

- Angry Put-Downs: "You're the stupidest person who ever lived."
- Abusive Recrimination: "You did it wrong, just like you always do."
- Competitiveness and Jealousy: see the Triangle later in this chapter.

- Physical Attack: spousal abuse, bar fights, road-rage fights, etc.

- Sarcasm: derived from the Greek word *sarkasmos*, meaning "to tear flesh."

- Hatred: expressed either verbally or by nasty treatment of the other.

- Sexual Sadism: lack of interest in the partner's satisfaction; taking the role of dominator/dominatrix in BDSM activity.

- Murder: the most extreme form of attack other behavior.

In Chapter 1, I offered four brief scenarios with lettered labels. The first was labeled "AO." It described the problem Tom had being grumpy and critical toward Alice, who had recently given birth to their first child. This is a very common happening in the lives of young couples. Alice's maternal focus on her newborn, coupled with her fatigue from nightly feedings and the other demands on the primary caretaker of an infant, was a natural impediment to her ability to show her interest in Tom. She did not love him any less. She simply had greater interest in meeting the needs of her baby. Tom had a natural shame reaction to this impediment in their emotional connection, but was unaware of its presence. As a result, he unconsciously defended himself from the vulnerable feelings shame caused with an *attack other* defense. There are many other situations in which attack other might arise. Here are several examples.

An *attack other* anecdote: A woman arrived home from work after picking up the couple's three children from day care. As soon as she saw her husband, she pointed a finger at him and said angrily, "We have to talk. You're in trouble!" He had an immediate shame reaction and was just about to attack back when he got hold of himself and calmly let the situation unfold. After they put the kids to bed, they sat down to talk about the incident. He discovered that during the drive home, the children had said they wished Mommy would go out that night, as she sometimes did with her girlfriends, and that Daddy would put them to bed. As she recounted the story, she admitted she felt mildly uncomfortable at first when the kids said they wanted her to go out. However, she found herself getting really mad when the kids said they would rather have Daddy put them to bed because he let them stay up later than Mommy and watch TV.

I had worked with this couple and they were well versed in affect psychology. As a result, they were able to decode her attack on him. It began when she felt mildly rejected—a shame reaction she did not recognize at first—because her kids said they preferred Daddy to her. It was compounded by the fact that she felt emotionally disconnected from him and hurt—another shame reaction—when the kids told her something that caused her to believe he violated an agreed-upon parental rule by letting them stay up late. They began to reconnect emotionally as they discussed the incident and her shame went completely away after he assured her that what the kids meant by staying up later was still well within the parameters they had agreed upon for bedtime.

An *attack other* scenario: In the last chapter, I briefly sketched a situation where someone comes home excited about a recent happening only to be "shushed" at the door by a partner engrossed in a TV show. If the shame reaction in the shushed partner is overly strong and attack other is their go-to defense, then one can easily imagine that person saying things like "That show is stupid, and so is anyone who watches it!" or "F— you! I'll be damned if I'm going to tell you the wonderful thing that just happened to me!"

Attack other* in therapy**: There are couples with whom I have worked in therapy where one, the other, or both might begin with a very loud "It's all his [or her] fault!" On the other hand, some attacks are more subtle, sometimes voiced as complaints or "I just have to say this one thing about what he (or she) does." I rapidly defuse such talk, stop the attack, and ask the attacker to examine his or her own shame. The bottom line is that such attacks are ***always a sign that the attacker is feeling shame. The emotional disconnection signaled by that shame can only be reestablished if the attacking person owns up to feeling vulnerable instead of disguising it by putting blame on the partner.

Some *attack other* at things scenarios: At the beginning of Chapter 2, I wrote about how I threw my golf clubs when frustrated on the golf course. For many years, I attempted to correct this behavior by working on my "anger" in therapy. It did not help. (In fact, I am somewhat legendary at my club for having once left four golf clubs stuck in a tree—one I tossed after I missed a shot from a sand trap and the other three in failed attempts to retrieve the first. And when I returned with my neighbor's ladder to fetch the clubs, a group of ladies playing that same hole, including a future club president, serenaded me with running commentary.)

I do not blame my therapist for why it took me so long to recognize the real affect involved. He was competent enough, but his mentors were versed primarily in psychoanalytic theory, hence he knew little or nothing about shame. As my understanding of shame evolved, and especially after Nathanson coined the term *attack other*, I began to see my anger in a different light. It became clear that it was a defense against shame. I was attacking the golf clubs as if it were their fault that I was playing poorly. My success rate at reducing the intensity of these negative emotions on the golf course has been much greater since I began working from the perspective that I was dealing with shame, not anger, whenever I missed a shot. (Notice that I did not say I *eliminated* my shame on the golf course. All golfers, including Tiger Woods, know that it is in the very nature of the game to create shame because it provides many and frequent impediments to one's interest in perfecting it.)

Golf clubs are far from the only objects of *attack other*. Have you ever kicked your car when it broke down? Or slammed a door that you bumped your head on? Or cursed at your knitting when you dropped a stitch? I once heard a news story about a woman in California who pulled a gun from her purse and shot the monitor after her computer froze for the millionth time. I am certain you can think of many times when you have attacked things either verbally or physically out of frustration. It is quite likely that you perceive attack other behaviors as motivated more by anger than by shame. While I will address this misconception in greater detail in the next chapter, the short version is that from early childhood we face impediments to our interest in doing things—the stimulus condition for the triggering of shame—and this makes us feel helpless again and again. Anger makes us feel less helpless. As the pattern "anger reducing helpless feelings" repeats over and over, we get better and better at it, and eventually it becomes second nature to ignore the helpless feelings and believe in the anger.

Attack Self Defenses
"I'm not OK."

At first glance, these shame defenses may seem like they would cause more shame, not reduce it. However, if one thinks of *attack self* as a compromise, it makes more sense. The compromise is that if I put myself down before anyone else does, then I, not you, control the amount of shame I feel. Not surprisingly, the early caregivers of people who, as adults, use attack self as their go-to defense mostly employed shame and attack other as their primary methods of socializing their children. The children therefore learn to put themselves down to help blunt their caregiver's attacks.

Here is a partial list of behaviors, each with a representative quote or thought, exhibited when shame is dealt with by the use of *attack self* methods of defense:

- Self-recrimination: "I am a complete screw up. I can't do anything right."
- Sexual Masochism: sexual activity with no interest or requests for the self being satisfied; taking the submissive role in BDSM activity.
- Self-mutilation: enough said.
- Suicide: the most extreme form of attack self behavior.

In the scenario I labeled "AS" in Chapter 1, I presented the story of Mindy and Matthew. Their emotional connection was impeded by Matthew's silence and inability to express his feelings openly. The shame triggered in Mindy by not knowing what was going on in Matthew's mind came from the impediment to intimacy caused by her not feeling any interest in her coming from him. Her shame made her feel stupid, ugly, fat, undesirable, and incompetent. She defended against the shame by attacking herself as the cause of the problem and putting herself down in his presence. Happily, this changed when therapy helped him become more open, especially because he learned how terrible she felt when he was not. Here are two more examples of attack self.

A typical *attack self* scenario: Someone you counted on to do something for you does not get the task done on time. As soon as you approach the person who has disappointed you, she or he begins immediately to regale you with what a loser, an idiot, and an irresponsible buffoon s/he is. The self put-down is so intense that you feel very uncomfortable about saying anything that might make them feel worse. Therefore, you say nothing that would shame them. That person, who really does feel legitimate shame about having let you down, has now controlled the interaction with you, preventing you from causing more shame.

Attack self in therapy settings: I have worked with many couples where one partner says "It's all my fault" and genuinely means it. This requires immediate intervention on the part of the therapist because the defense blocks emotional connection if it goes unchallenged.

Withdrawal Defenses
"I'm outta here!"
This group of shame defenses works by removing us from situations that cause shame. It is often a relatively straightforward defense. The per-

son is aware that shame is present or might be present and withdraws into their house or room or into their own head. They keep their real feelings to themselves for fear that anything they expose will be stupid or silly, or will in some way open them up to ridicule by others. They have great fear (fear of shame) that others will see them—literally and figuratively—as defective; as a result, they prefer to hide both their inmost, emotional self and their physical self.

Here is a partial list of behaviors, each with a representative quote or thought, exhibited when someone deals with shame by the use of *withdrawal* methods of defense:

- Solo Activity: often becomes a lifestyle choice in "shy" people.

- Silence: a serious, impenetrable impediment to emotional connection.

- Sexual Withdrawal: can be through impotence, frigidity, or never approaching one's partner.

- Agoraphobia: the most serious form can be crippling for reaching life's goals.

Although withdrawal defenses may not need an anecdote for further clarification, the following self-revelation is an excellent example. My great friend, former college roommate, and fishing partner Ronald Denis, who has been blind since age fourteen months, sent me the following:

The problem with being blind is that one often has trouble knowing for sure whether or not one is being addressed. I find that whether or not I respond to someone saying something like "Hello" or "Nice day, isn't it?" (a common occurrence here in the south whether or not one knows the speaker) depends on what happened the last time something similar happened to me. If the last person who I responded to was actually talking to me, I respond to anyone who might be addressing me. If, however, the last person to whom I responded was not talking to me, I do not respond to the current person. I don't think about this; it just seems to be how I automatically respond. Whatever strategy is involved, it consists of doing what worked last until it doesn't, then reversing course until the new strategy fails. (In truth, this is partially mood related, as when I'm in a particularly good mood, I respond to everything, no matter what. That this includes birds, trees, and whatever else I encounter is sometimes viewed with concern by those within hearing range.)

Ron, whose great sense of humor is one reason I love him, consciously withdraws by not responding after incidents that cause him shame. This is caused, in part, by the enhanced hearing skills he's developed to compensate for his blindness. When we walk down the street together, I can see him attending to conversations that I can hear only partially or not at all. He often hears quite clearly the private conversations of people talking to one another at so-called normal, socially acceptable volumes. If one conversant does not respond to the other quickly enough, Ron sometimes perceives the last sentence as addressed to him, leaving him in the dilemma of whether or not to respond.

The "W" scenario presented in Chapter 1 is an example of withdrawal. As Sally began to work longer and longer hours, Sarah experienced shame because the time apart was an impediment to their intimacy. For Sarah, the most prominent shame emotions were feelings of loneliness and isolation. She could not open up about this to Sally because she knew that Sally had no control over her schedule. Sally was already exhausted and unhappy about her extended hours, and Sarah did not want to do anything to make her feel worse than she already did. Sarah thought she was strong enough to handle the lonely feelings by herself. But as time passed, her withholding of those feelings began to affect all of her feelings for Sarah, causing her to become more and more withdrawn.

As evidenced by Sarah and Sally's situation, typical *withdrawal* scenarios for the most part involve not talking to one's partner or removing oneself from the other's presence—behaviors we have all used after having a marital spat because they momentarily reduce bad feelings. Such momentary silences or going to another room in the house can serve a very useful purpose because they help reduce the intensity of shame and anger. At times, this allows us to recover our emotional balance enough to be able to re-approach our partner with more positive affect and less vulnerable feelings. When, on the other hand, the shame is too intense or goes on too long, then more serious withdrawal behaviors arise. Partners can experience such things as complete lack of interest in or willingness to engage in sexual activity, no desire to spend time together, and long, long periods of silence when together—one woman told me the story of a nine-hour drive to see their child at college during which her husband spoke, and she counted, fewer than ten words.

Withdrawal **in therapy settings**: Usually this involves one partner who says little if anything during the session. However, on three occasions in my work with couples, intense shame in one of the partners motivated them to jump to their feet and leave the office in the middle of the hour.

Avoidance Defenses

"I don't know what you're talking about, and neither do you!"

This group of shame defenses uses various forms of denial to handle the feelings arising from shame. The denial is an attempt to remove feelings of shame, in whole or in part, from conscious awareness. People who use avoidance defenses frequently have patterns that also promote the use of attack other, especially if their denial is confronted. When avoidance behaviors become a person's constant companion, seemingly part of their character, it gives rise to people with "big egos," with rigidly judgmental opinions of others, with extremely limited knowledge of all their feelings, not just shame, and an apparent lack of insight into their own faults. These are people who cannot be wrong because they know they are always "right."

Here is a partial list of behaviors, each with a representative quote or thought, exhibited when someone deals with shame by the use of *avoidance* methods of defense:

- Machoism: "Me, weak in any way? You can't be serious. But if you don't shut your mouth right now, I'll shut it for you." (avoidance plus attack other)

- Workaholism: "I would love to spend more time with my family, but I have so much work and so many people are depending on me that I just cannot get away from the office."

- Alcoholism and Drug Abuse: as I have heard Dr. Nathanson say in hundreds of lectures on the Compass of Shame, "Shame is soluble in drugs and alcohol."

- Over-intellectualization: particularly prevalent in those who've had so much education—like lawyers, doctors, professors of all kinds, especially in philosophy, psychologists, and engineers—that they know they know more than you and that they are right and you are probably wrong because you're not logical enough; you're too emotional.

- Competitiveness and Jealousy: see the Triangle later in this chapter.

- Multiple Plastic Surgeries: as if constantly getting the body and face reshaped will really combat the effects of aging.

- Obsessive Wealth Gathering: covering up any signs of being lesser or defective with everything money can buy, including the use of money to control others, have them look up to and kowtow to you so that you "know" you are important.

- Verbal Gibberish: just going on and on and on and on and on and on, so that no one can really see what's underneath all the talk.

- Sexual Infidelity: "I just can't help it, these other women want me."

The "A" scenario presented in Chapter 1 described the problem of Harry's drinking too much when his in-laws came to visit. There were several factors at work here. The first was that his in-laws were very intrusive people. When they came to visit, they virtually took over all conversation and frequently interrupted Harry when he attempted to add something. This created shame in Harry, who already felt some shame that he had had to borrow money from them to help pay for his children's college educations. A more subtle effect of their visit was that it temporarily impeded the newfound emotional intimacy between Betty and him, triggering uncomfortable feelings of distance in the relationship. As a result, Harry drank more than usual to make the shame go away.

Typical *avoidance* scenarios: One of the most common types in heterosexual relationships is related to the misconception among many men that they are primarily logical beings and that woman are illogical, emotional beings. This misconception is supported by our biological differences and cultural demands that women be one way and men another, factors that create somewhat different emotional patterns in men and women. While the sexes may seem different and behave different emotionally, all human beings are born with the same nine innate affects, and those affects underlie all motivation (see Appendix I for more details). The typical scene based on this misconception, and played over and over again in many relationships, is that of a man with hurt, inferior, rejected, weak, or other shame-based feelings hidden—to both himself and his wife—behind a spuriously logical lecture to his wife about how if she would only be less "emotional" or would just "calm down," they would have a better relationship. His denial of his vulnerability is an impenetrable impediment to emotional connection.

Other behaviors that arise from shame avoidance defenses include, but are not restricted to: the drinker who comes home every night and drinks himself to sleep; the chronic marijuana smoker who avoids most of life, lost in an alteration of his senses that keeps him stuck inside his own head; the philosophy professor or engineer-type person who lectures his partner in unemotional tones; the adversarial, lawyer-like person who debates everything brought up by his or her partner; and the macho, John Wayne type who charges forward at all costs, never admitting to or showing any weakness.

Avoidance **in therapy settings**: This usually involves intellectualizations and rationalizations that constantly deny all vulnerable feelings, especially shame. I well remember a session in 1995 with a father—a brilliant architect—and his high-achieving college-age daughter. This session was part of a series of meetings to discuss the utter inability of the daughter and her stepmother, who had no biological children of her own, to live in harmony. The daughter complained in her individual sessions that whenever she was emotional, her father's sole response was to tell her to "calm down." When I explained the issues related to shame that drove the negative affect between stepmother and child, and how his own vulnerability placed him in a compromising position between the two, this man who had absolutely no background or training in psychological matters, nor had he been in therapy himself, quietly opined that I was very wrong. After a brief dissertation on his theory of human psychology that proved, at least to him, that he had no vulnerability whatsoever in this matter, he went on to say that it was not his feelings about what was going on that caused him to intervene. Instead, he quietly insisted that it was only logical in this situation that he teach both his daughter and his wife how to be more logical with one another. At which point his daughter interrupted and said, "See what I mean!" (It will come as no surprise to you that this man grew up with a mother who was an unruly, emotional volcano who attacked him regularly with shaming words. With his brilliant mind and such strong motivation to do so, he developed the avoidance technique of supreme logic to get away from all emotion.)

A Triangle

Some years ago, Don Nathanson and I collaborated on a book about shame only to have it rejected by at least a dozen publishing houses. The shame triggered by these rejections caused me to abandon writing for a time and take to the golf course. It caused Don to intensify his search of the world's literature about shame, propelling him to the status of the leading expert on the topic and the publication of *Shame and Pride*. In other words, I used withdrawal and he used avoidance through intellectualization to deal with our shame. The choice of these different defenses is traceable to a significant difference in our families of origin. Don's family worshipped the intellectual achievements of Nobel Prize winners. My family worshipped Arnold Palmer.

It is worth noting again that defenses against shame are necessary, especially when we are little kids and mostly powerless in relation to those around us. Moreover, those defenses—despite some of the negative behaviors outlined earlier in this chapter—do not always lead to "bad" things. I quite enjoy being able to play golf as a single-digit handicapper, and Don's work has illuminated for many the significance of shame, familiarity with which is necessary for anyone seeking in-depth knowledge of the self. (As many now know, Descartes was wrong. It is not enough to say, "Cogito, ergo sum," or "I think, therefore I am." Instead, it is more accurate, but less easy, to say, "I am made consciously aware of the world outside and inside of me because I have affects, and if I think about those affects and how they affect my thinking, I know who I am." The shorter version of this would be: "I feel, therefore I am," or possibly "Sentio, ergo sum.")

One of the discoveries Don and I made while working on the rejected book was the frequency with which competitiveness, jealousy, and shame are interrelated. To represent the fact that where you find one, you very frequently find the other two, we adopted the image of a triangle. I am sure that this was partly motivated by our experience treating people involved in so-called love triangles, where jealousy, competitiveness, and shame can be found in abundance. The dynamic in a love triangle is that if I love you, but you love him—or even *seem* to love him—more than you love me, then that is an impediment to my interest in you loving me and me loving you. Because of this impediment, shame is triggered in me (experienced as feeling rejected, hurt, and distanced by you), and that makes me jealous of him. As long as I still love you, I will have that shame, and in my attempt to minimize it, I will compete with him in order to "win" you back. Therefore, I will try to be smarter, stronger, funnier, richer, more handsome, or somehow a better person than he so that you will love me more.

Furthermore, while competing with him, I may become "jealous" of your every move. (I often hear people use the word "paranoid" when discussing this. Paranoia is a shame-motivated phenomenon. For the purpose of this discussion, think of paranoia as an intense form of jealousy, motivated by intense shame.) If you are quiet, I may think you are thinking of him. If you are not home on time, I may think you are with him. If your phone is busy, I may think you are talking to him, and in this day and age of cellular phones, I may scour the pages of the phone record of all your calls, looking for his phone number. (I had one patient tell me that he thought his wife was too clever to use her cell phone to call a number he might recognize. To counter that, he placed a small tracking device in her phone. Each day he would compare the computer records of where she had been with her stories of what she had done that day. Eventually he tracked her to a place she frequented regularly but never mentioned. Unfortunately, he discovered her there with his best friend, the best man at their wedding, with whom she'd been having an affair since before they were married. Moral: Some jealousy and paranoia is right on the money.)

Because the intensity of shame reactions is directly proportional to the intensity of the interest or enjoyment impeded, it is generally the case that the intensity of the shame one feels in a love triangle is directly proportional to how strong one's love is at the moment. However, we each enter into adult love relationships with different levels of vulnerability to shame based on childhood experience, as well as on what has transpired in our prior love relationships. People with low self-esteem carry much more shame vulnerability into their relationships and are, therefore, prone to much more intense shame reactions if a love triangle develops. The greater the shame, the greater the jealous and competitive behaviors will be. If jealousy and/or competitiveness are extremely intense, they become successful combinations of *attack other* and *avoidance* defenses, diverting one away from the shame that motivates them. The concept of the triangle, a representation of which is below to give you a visual image to remember, helps one keep in mind that **where you find one, you find the other two**.

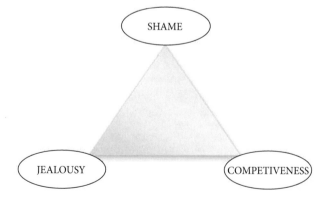

While we usually think of jealousy in a negative light, many in our culture not only think of competitiveness in a positive light, they revere or even worship it. You might ask, "Is competitiveness always motivated by shame? Is competitiveness a bad thing? The answer to the first question is yes, and to the second, no. In response to the first question, consider what Nathanson wrote in *Shame and Pride* (page 351):

> Since so much of our self-concept is derived from comparison with others, and since it is through the medium of competition that we set up purposeful systems of comparison, it stands to reason that shame stemming from some perceived but irremediable deficiency of the self can be mitigated by shifting attention toward the pride and status achieved when one wins at something. Directly proportional to the amount of energy devoted to competition is always the degree of chronic shame linked to a persistently lowered self-image.

In competitiveness related to sports, for instance, one can attack the foe with the intention of "beating" him or "crushing" him or "thrashing" him to prove that the winner is not weak or inferior. We all know people who cannot stop themselves from being competitive in virtually everything they do. Whether it is about their athletic performance, the way they look, the money they make, or about every little thing we say that they feel compelled to debate, they appear to be constantly in competitive modes of behavior.

We have all felt little, helpless, and weak many times in our lives. That shame motivates us to rid ourselves of these feelings is simply a result of the way we are wired. In many respects, this is not a good or bad thing; it simply **is**! Using competitive means to reduce feelings of vulnerability arising from shame is something everyone does. As is the case with most human behaviors, there are competitive behaviors that are creative, healthy, and useful not only to the person engaged in them but also to those around him. The art of intimacy, in fact, is often enhanced by the fun two people can have competing at cards, tennis, golf, board games, intellectual debates, and anything else under the sun. On the other hand, the behaviors of a person locked in a lifelong struggle to overcome shame from "a persistently lowered self-image" usually impede emotional connection with others. Competing with such folks is never fun. They make you feel awful in the process of beating you, and heaven forbid they should lose; they make you feel awful that you beat them.

A final note about the triangle: In what may be their worst manifestation, jealousy and competitiveness can combine to form the need for revenge. This only happens when the shame experienced is at levels of great intensity and at the humiliation to mortification end of the scale. Revenge carried out using *attack other* can result in murder, and many disastrous love triangles have ended this way. If the revenge causes someone to revert to *attack self*, suicides can occur based on the distorted thought: "I'll kill myself and then you'll be sorry." And, of course, there are the murder-suicides that combine both attack other and attack self modes of acting out the revenge.

In less serious cases, people often become stuck with thoughts of revenge that never leave them. These thoughts can dominate their thinking, their way of perceiving situations, and control their lives. In other words, they firmly believe that getting some kind of revenge is the only way they will feel better. They are wrong in this belief. They can only feel better if they do something about their shame. If revenge permanently disguises their feelings of shame, preventing them from doing work on the self to reduce shame, they will never feel better.

For example, I've worked in therapy with a number of people who were obsessed with getting revenge against an ex-spouse. What was not obvious to them was that they really had two shame-related problems. The first was the shame triggered by the spouse's behavior, whether it was because of affairs, abusive treatment, or an unceremonious dumping for a younger model. The second was deeper shame within the self resulting from damage done them before they met their spouse. Being stuck in revenge (attack other) mode prevented several of them from dealing with their own negative sense of self, and revenge became an emotional cancer from which they never recovered.

Shame-jealousy-competitiveness triangles begin at a very early age. Freud called this the Oedipus Complex and Jung called it the Electra Complex when the scripts involved related to a child's parents. Children get into triangles with others besides their parents as the picture on the next page clearly illustrates.

Photo by Furman Baldwin

SUMMARY

It is absolutely, categorically, unbelievably, out-of-this-world critical that you become skilled at recognizing behaviors that disguise or cover up shame **IF** you are going to be able to use the information presented in this book to help you maintain a positive balance in your emotional connection with your significant other—or anyone else, for that matter, including yourself.

The Triangle should be easy to remember, although you may at times have trouble convincing yourself that jealousy and competitiveness always relate to shame issues. But because it is somewhat more complex, if you find the Compass of Shame less intuitive, please page back and look at it again for visual reinforcement. Since it is the nature of all relationships to have moments when shame is triggered, and since shame can easily ruin your relationship, to get the most out of what I offer in these pages, I encourage you to study behavior in yourself and others to determine if it resides on one of the four poles of the Compass of Shame.

CHAPTER 7

YOUR ANGER IS LYING TO YOU

All violent feelings have the same effect. They produce in us a falseness in all our impressions of external things, which I would generally characterize as the "pathetic fallacy." [2]

While I might use the word "tragic" in place of "pathetic" as the English art critic, poet, artist, and social thinker John Ruskin did in this quote from an 1856 treatise, I certainly agree with his opinion as it applies to anger. When violently angry, the emotion distorts our ability to perceive accurately and interpret what is going on around us. Perhaps you have heard sayings such as "an angry man can't learn" or "an angry man can't teach." Anger, especially at greater levels of intensity, short-circuits our brains and leads us to do and say things we would never do or say when not angry. One of the reasons professional boxers often do everything possible to get their opponents angry—and "The Greatest," Muhammad Ali, was a master at provoking an opponent's rage—is because an angry boxer forgets all the defensive technique he practiced during months of training and is then vulnerable to the knock-out punch.

But an even greater tragedy is the overly frequent promotion of anger as the root cause of problems and problematic behaviors by the many psychological theorists and practitioners who remain stuck in Freudian-like theories of motivation based on notions about the presence of some mysterious force called the "aggressive drive." Yes, anger is loud, often very visible, and a precursor to violent behaviors. But, while there is no question the reduction of anger in individuals or cultures will increase harmonious relationships between people and nations, accomplishing this feat within the current belief system is impossible. Too many do not understand that anger is an inherited, completely natural feeling state. It is triggered in everyone whenever the brain reaches a condition best described as "overload" because someone is immersed in too much hap-

---

2. From "Of the Pathetic Fallacy" by John Ruskin in *Modern Painters*, volume iii, pt. 4, 1856.

pening for too long at too dense a level of stimulus density (for more details, see "A Primer of Affect Psychology" in Appendix I). In other words, anger is a normal response when certain things happen to us. While some people may act like animals when enraged, anger itself is not some wild, dark, mysteriously triggered demon from within.

The way those who work with affect psychology think about anger is that some very real event must happen first before anger is set off. It is true that some people's anger triggers more easily than others. This is simply information about their preexisting emotional state. Whether it is for psychological or biological reasons, such people are already close to being on overload emotionally. If, for instance, I ask you to step into a small, locked room and listen to music you do not like at a volume uncomfortable for you, how long it takes you to become angry will depend on how you were feeling ahead of time. If you were feeling well rested and had little on your mind, it might take you quite some time before you had "had enough" and begin angrily pounding on the door to be let out. However, if you were feeling a bit ill or had a great deal else on your mind or were exhausted at the end of a long day—in other words, if you were already experiencing distress—your anger would probably be tripped much sooner.

The take-home point is that it is a much more accurate conceptualization of anger to think of it as a natural response to real things rather than as a morally reprehensible animal residing inside of certain unfortunate people. Thought of this way, it is easier to trace the natural history of how anger becomes a "fallacy." Before doing that, however, I ask that you think back about your own emotional reactions for a minute. Can you remember times when you felt weak or helpless or stupid or afraid and then became angry or enraged? Didn't the anger feel much better than the weak, helpless, stupid, or fearful state you were in? Wasn't it preferable to pump some adrenaline, clench your fists, or yell rather than feel those disabling vulnerable feelings? Of course it was, even if you became embarrassed about the angry outburst afterwards. Why does being angry make most of us feel not only less vulnerable, but sometimes invulnerable?

There is no clear-cut answer to this question. Perhaps it evolved as a survival mechanism. What, for instance, is our chance for survival if when confronted by a wild beast we simply remain frozen in fear? If instead we get angry, we may pick up a rock or stick, scream at the beast, fight it head-on, and perhaps save ourselves. Regardless of the reason why it evolved, simply put, anger feels less bad than those other feelings. Therefore, it can function as a protection against feeling helpless. (Anger and fear are the motivating forces that direct the formation of the well-known "flight or fight" response pattern.)

Once you come to appreciate the fact that anger feels less bad than fear, distress, and shame, it becomes easier to understand how I arrived at the title of this chapter. Anger is a "lie" not because someone is faking being angry—the anger is quite genuine—but because of anger's role as a diversionary tactic. Its intent is to trick both the self and others into believing we are neither weak nor vulnerable. For instance, when somebody is really angry at you, can you see or feel anything else about them but their anger? No: anger is an enormously effective fallacy. It deflects attention—both yours and theirs—away from other things going on inside them. If we really want to understand what motivates angry behaviors, we must conceive of anger not as a cause, but as symptomatic of underlying feelings of vulnerability, especially of shame. Affect psychologists think of it this way:

Feelings of fear or distress or shame immediately precede almost every angry moment.

The bad news about anger is that once labeled as an "angry person," it is too easy for that person, and for others, to ignore the real cause of their problems or to see their vulnerability. Specifically for this book about relationships, the bad news about anger is that it blocks emotional connection. It is virtually impossible to feel emotionally intimate with someone whose vulnerable self remains hidden behind anger. Furthermore, anger has an extremely contagious nature, almost always inducing similar degrees of anger in one's partner. Once both people are angry, the stage is set for the angry, attack other Compass of Shame spirals discussed in the next chapter.

The Scripting of Anger

In the second chapter, I briefly described how adult *emotions* come into being. It starts at birth, and there is a continual interplay from that time onward between our nine innate affects, our inborn temperament, and the personalities of our caregivers. Through learning, we adjust our natural affective responses—our natural inborn feelings—to the demands of our environment. Eventually the natural display of feelings, so readily visible on the faces and in the body language of small children, morphs into a series of learned (or what those who work with affect script psychology call *scripted*) responses.

For example, the scripted **emotion** *anger* in someone who grew up in an environment where it was acceptable to display anger by yelling, screaming, shouting, and shaking one's fist is going to be very different from that of someone who grew up around people who only displayed a tight-lipped silence when angry. When angry as adults, these two people will seem very different **emotionally,** even if they are experiencing anger at the same level of intensity. And these differences are further amplified in women versus men because anger scripts form in the presence of differences in biology—musculature, hormones, brains, etc.—and the demands differentially imposed on girls and boys by the disparate demands of the cultures in which they grow up.

While the display of the **emotion** anger ends up looking somewhat different in different people, most of the time, we can tell if someone is angry. The exceptions to this rule involve people who have been so severely shamed or terrified as children that they have been forced to protect themselves by completely suppressing or hiding any outward display of anger. The scripts of such people incorporate traits such as passive-aggressive behavior or stony-faced responses, making it difficult both for us and for them to know what they are really feeling. This presents a serious problem for maintaining emotional connection that I will address in a later chapter. The hiding of anger is one form of deception or "lie," but such scripts are not the point of this chapter. Instead, I am trying to paint a picture about the deceptive nature of clearly recognizable displays of anger.

Given that anger is less toxic, less uncomfortable, than fear, distress, or shame, how does it jump in and replace those feelings in order to create the illusion that we are more powerful and less helpless than we really feel? The earliest scripting of this begins at birth and is initiated, without conscious thought, as a normal consequence of our biological inheritance. The natural cry of distress when an infant is hungry is familiar to all of us. So too is the situation where something happens to that cry when babies are ignored for too long. It changes to a more intense tone and usually increases in volume, often prompting the caregiver to say, "Oh, she's mad at me now."

The cry of distress becomes the howl of rage when the central nervous system reaches a state of too, too much (or overload) caused by intensification of the distress.

In the case of hunger demands not met soon enough, the unrelieved hunger continually retriggers more and more distress, and then the distress triggers more distress, creating a normal, natural progression to anger. This is simply a matter of the way our brains are wired. Stated another way: Anger is a natural outcome when distress becomes too overwhelming. Since it is impossible—nor is it the best thing for the child's development—for a caregiver to always arrive at the first cry of distress, the sequence of distress becoming anger occurs time and time again in early childhood. With many repetitions, there are several reasons why it becomes highly probable that the infant will "learn" (become scripted) to become angry sooner and sooner after the distress begins. Perhaps the most important reason from an inter-affective perspective is that the howl of anger is more distressing to caregivers than the cry of distress and therefore more likely to motivate them to respond sooner. The quicker the caregiver responds to a behavior, the more the infant will replicate that behavior to elicit that response.

I also suspect—although it is essentially impossible to prove—that, not unlike adults, even very young infants experience anger as a less helpless feeling state than distress and begin to prefer the angry state over the distressed state. This is consistent with the normal function of the brain's Central Blueprint to **minimize** negative feelings. In this case, it is a compromise between anger and distress. Anger wins out because it makes one feel less helpless. Even if this is not true for very young infants, it certainly becomes true as we get older.

Eventually there will develop scripts where distress is so short-lived, it appears to all but the highly attuned observer that the child was only angry, never distressed. Furthermore, once one learns the script of "anger to reduce helpless feelings caused by distress," it generalizes to other feelings that create a sense of helplessness, namely fear and shame. Anger scripts can make those feelings all but "disappear" also. (The need by some theorists to postulate the presence of an "aggressive drive" is most likely the result of their lack of awareness of innate affects and this scripting process. Virtually all "aggressive" behaviors of which they speak are motivated from within anger scripts.)

When I was training in psychiatry, it was generally accepted that anger was a critical factor in mental illness and emotional disorders. By then, many in the mental health professions and the general public understood the necessity of becoming aware of one's anger and expressing it. One had to "get anger out" to avoid having it turn inward and attack the self, causing depression as well as other physical illnesses. Popular techniques for unearthing and expressing anger included such things as encouraging people to punch pillows. In couples therapy, the therapist would give someone suspected of being angry but suppressing it a large padded bat and instructions to hit their partner. There is a hilarious parody of these techniques in the 1999 Hollywood comedy *Analyze This*. The psychiatrist, played by Billy Crystal, wants his depressed mafia boss patient, played by Robert De Niro, to get his anger out. He suggests hitting a pillow. Feeling silly at the thought of "hitting" a pillow, the mafia boss refuses. When the psychiatrist insists, the patient suddenly pulls out a gun and fires several shots into the pillow. After recovering from the shock of sudden gunfire, the psychiatrist asks, "Feel better?" To which the mafia boss replies, "Yeah, I do."

I have never questioned the mental health profession's focus on anger and the need to be aware of the clear-cut dangers anger poses to mental and physical health. Because my training occurred in an era during which anger was incompletely understood, I spent a great deal of time early in my career helping folks become aware of anger and expressing it. The problem I encountered was that all too frequently this did not help my patients solve any problems or develop a more comfortable relationship with their anger. I had to face the disappointing and embarrassing fact that my training had left me with an incomplete knowledge of human motivation. Further study led me to affect psychology where I discovered the missing pieces—the essential role of the nine innate affects for motivation, emotion, and cognition. I was excited to learn affect motivates *everything*, including more affect.

As a result of this new perspective, I changed and my therapy style changed. I still help people become aware of their anger, but I do not spend much time, if any, having them "get their anger out" by punching pillows or yelling at their spouses. Not only does it not solve anything, it often increases the anger (in both people) and creates shame. I ask instead, "Why do you think it was **anger** that you felt in this situation?" Their frequent defensive response (because they feel shame about their anger) is: "Wouldn't anybody get angry in that situation?" Once we get past the defensiveness, I ask them to look at and share with me the slow-motion instant replay of the moments leading up to the anger. It is *always* the case that something(s) did happen emotionally before the anger was triggered.

This here-and-now focus on feelings and motivation creates a new understanding of the vulnerable side of the self. It often leads people to explore old memories of past feelings of vulnerability and how their anger scripts evolved from those moments of helplessness. When people see their anger as primarily a defensive maneuver to protect them from distress, fear, or shame, they feel less shame about their anger and are therefore less likely to become immersed in the spiral of shame leading to anger leading to more shame and the need for more anger and so on.

RANT: *Any therapeutic intervention for reducing anger that does not reduce shame about anger is useless!*

RANT: *Any theory about anger that does not recognize the vulnerable feelings of distress, fear, and shame underlying the anger is utterly incomplete!*

Now that I've gotten that off my chest, I feel much better. Deep breath…deep breath…ahhh.

In a personal communication in March 2010, Donald Nathanson told me that his research findings indicate that shame precedes anger approximately 90% of the time. Before examining this most common reason for anger scripts, here are a few examples of anger defending against distress and fear—although in fairness, on close examination, if one is looking for it, one sees something from the shame family of emotions in every example.

Anger Defending Distress (and Shame)

An exaggerated but not implausible scenario: Harry is on his way to work. He's late. He's tired because he had to stay up well past midnight preparing for the meeting scheduled that morning. His mind, not fully awake, is filled with thoughts of all the things he has to do, as well as the difficult and unwanted decisions that will be forced on him in the meeting. He has plenty of time to ruminate on these things because traffic is moving so slowly that he has gone only one mile in the last fifteen minutes, thus guaranteeing that he will be late for the meeting. As his cell phone rings for the fifth time with another call from his assistant asking the same silly question again, he spills the last drops of his coffee on the extravagantly expensive new suit purchased the day before so he would look his most dignified and self-assured self at the meeting.

What happens next? In most versions of this story, an enraged Harry begins yelling at his assistant. Harry is clearly under what most people would call a lot of "stress." (Whenever you hear the word "stress," if you wish to fine-tune your awareness of feelings, I suggest you interpret it as meaning that the person experiencing it is feeling *distress.*) It is difficult to imagine anyone in Harry's situation who would not be in distress. The final phone call and spilling the coffee on his suit sends his central nervous system into a state of complete overload, and anger is triggered. It is just too much to bear. I think most people would consider it "normal" to get angry in this situation. I know I do. The more **continual** pressure on us from internal sources (thoughts or unpleasant bodily sensations) or external sources (work, traffic, school, etc.), the greater our distress and the closer we are to overload, and therefore, the closer we are to anger.

As is true in most situations of this nature, shame is also at work. His feeling ashamed at being late for an important meeting, his sense of help-lessness being stuck in traffic, his embarrassment at his soiled suit, and his frustration with his assistant's inability to understand what he needs to have done have all contributed to Harry's feelings of shame. Harry's defensive anger, therefore, becomes an attack other response directed at his assistant.

The take-home message from poor Harry's dilemma is: When you find yourself or your partner getting angry, look beyond the anger to see if you or she is in distress. Anything that produces too much for too long will trigger distress. Be particularly attuned to persistent physical pain as a source of distress. One of my patients is married to a woman with severe rheumatoid arthritis. Her joint pain and the restriction on her movement caused by the illness make it impossible for her to dress her-self. In spite of this, she courageously goes to work every day. She is often irritable and easily angered while he helps her get dressed for work. He uses his knowledge of affect psychology to help him remain calm when she is angry because he sees the high level of distress beneath the anger. And—here is shame again—he is highly attuned to her growing sense of helplessness (shame) as her disease progresses.

Anger Defending Fear (and Shame)

Working in therapy with the parents of teenagers—and having been a parent of two teenagers myself—the issue of getting angry at kids who stay out too late or past parentally imposed curfews comes up repeatedly. Parents who are attuned to their feelings and willing to look past their anger realize that there are two strong emotions behind the anger. The first is the fear that their child will be harmed or (a parent's most terrify-ing nightmare) killed because the teenager is inexperienced and because we were all teenagers once and know from firsthand experience the stu-pid, reckless things teenagers do. The second is the helpless (shame) feel-ing of not knowing where the child is, who the child is with, or what the child is doing—exacerbated by the fact that just a few years before, we were completely in control of the whereabouts, companions, and actions of our kids. There can also be shame feelings and a sense of rejection that one's child is now more interested in others outside of the family. Even though we "know" it is healthy for our kids to have friends and become more independent of us, we still feel a bit hurt as they gradually withdraw their interest in us.

Here is a not uncommon scenario: A teenager is late. As the hour the teenager should have been home comes and goes, at first the parent feels some fear and helplessness. However, as time passes, there is a growing annoyance, and then outright anger replaces the fear. Has it then happened to you that when your teenager finally called or came in the door, the very first words out of your mouth were a loud, clipped, angrily spoken, "Where have you been?!"? Parents not attuned to their vulnerable affects end up getting into frequent angry battles with their teenagers, forcing their children to withdraw even further. (These scenes are more deleterious if these same parents have unresolved shame that keeps them locked into controlling scripts.) Parents who are attuned share their fears to avoid serious damage to the emotional connection with their kids.

Many incidents of so-called *road rage* also belong in the category of fear defended by anger. I have carried out an informal research program looking into this phenomenon. I asked hundreds of people the following question: "What do you do immediately after another driver does something that scares you, such as cutting too closely in front of you at high speed?" Almost 100% of the responses involve anger in some form. The majority of the responses indicate that the angry response was mild with some short-lived, angrily voiced words and a few derogatory hand gestures. The angriest responses—the ones that would be truly considered road rage—were given mostly by men who have more deeply imbedded shame issues and show signs of shame, jealousy, and competitiveness in many areas of their lives. These men report responding to the moment of helpless fear by chasing after the offending person, tailgating them or cutting back in front of them at high speeds, often while yelling and displaying the middle finger. (Another mini rant: Too many conceive of road rage as being only about anger. This is a serious mistake because it is unlikely to help those who become involved in such incidents, and that is dangerous for all of us who drive.)

Anger Scripts Defending Shame

The innate affect shame is just that, innate. We are born with it and with its function of signaling impediment to interest and enjoyment. Small children face many impediments to their interests. For instance, until they are able to walk, it is difficult or impossible for them to reach interesting things they see at a distance. Until they grow taller, it is difficult or impossible for them to reach interesting things they see on shelves or countertops. Until they develop understandable hand signals or speech, it is also difficult for them to make their interests known to those who can help further or remove impediments to those interests.

Newborn infants are very distractible but become less so as their brains mature. This initial distractibility and the fact that everything to them is so novel—the primary trigger of interest—essentially eliminates the problem caused by impediments. They shift fluidly from one item of interest to the next. As they develop, however, the impediments of being too weak, too small, and too helpless begin to trigger significant amounts of shame. The item from the shame family of emotions they most commonly exhibit is **frustration**, which, as every parent knows only too well, becomes outright anger rather easily. Here begins the formation of the script of "anger defending against shame." Paradoxically, if they have primarily positive relationships with their caregivers, whom they have learned will help them reduce negative feelings, they direct this frustration and anger toward those caregivers—an example of the "attack other" pole of the Compass of Shame.

Here is an example: When my grandson Collin was between 30 and 36 months old, I observed the following scene. We were in my daughter's kitchen on a very pleasant afternoon. There had been no negative emotion; everyone was playing well together. Collin was walking around the kitchen exhibiting a normal child's interest in picking up and touching everything in sight. At the same time, he was interacting positively with his sister, mother, grandmother, and me. I saw his eyes catch a glimpse of a shiny object on the kitchen counter. His interest focused on this new thing, but it was out of his reach. He took a step toward the counter and stopped, his head sagged almost imperceptibly, and then he hit his mother, even though she was not blocking his path to the object of his interest. My daughter handled the incident gracefully with appropriate limits. She did not overly shame him for his behavior, and, as a result, the positive feelings of the afternoon were disrupted for only a minute or two and then everyone went back to enjoying the visit. This is a clear example of impeded interest triggering the innate affect shame. Collin was old enough to have experienced many such incidents and to have in place anger scripts to deal with helpless feelings. As a result, he resorted to an attack other moment of anger. This is so common in children that I have been tempted to label it "attack **mother**."

I encourage you to observe anger in young children from this new perspective. If their primary caregivers have been appropriately attentive to their needs, you will see many instances during which the child is "angry" or "aggressive" toward the caregiver. This can be very worrisome and handled improperly if one does not understand the true motivation behind the angry behavior. If, for instance, one interprets the anger as a demonic force inside the child, he is likely to be punished using extremely punitive measures. Such treatment may engender sufficient fear in the child that he stops the behavior. However, such measures also teach the child that HE is a demon instead of providing him with information about his emotions that he can use to his betterment. (Children who believe they are demons develop unmanageable levels of internalized shame. Their personalities evolve with the constant need to defend against feelings of shame, which engenders the need to develop defensive scripts at the extreme ends of the Compass of Shame. They then become too attacking of self or others, or too withdrawn, or too enmeshed in avoidance behaviors like alcoholism.)

Regardless of how well or how poorly caregivers manage a child's anger, however, everyone develops anger scripts to defend against shame. Discussion of the determinants of whether one's anger scripts are mild in intensity or involve dangerous levels of rage is beyond the scope of this book. (A DVD entitled *Managing Shame, Preventing Violence* is an excellent reference for the study of destructive anger scripts in Western culture. It is available at www.tomkins.org.)

SUMMARY

Almost all anger and its accompanying behaviors are scripted from early childhood to defend us against feelings that are more vulnerable. One cannot solve problems created by anger without attending to the fear, distress, or shame that lies hidden beneath the anger. Misconceptions about anger and its meanings are a major contributor to the hidden challenge of shame.

Emotional connection and intimacy are impossible in the presence of anger. We must have access to the vulnerable feelings, especially the shame experienced by our partner, if we are going to resolve issues related to emotional disconnection. The next chapter focuses on the negative consequences for relationships of not having access to those feelings.

The problems created by anger extend well beyond the disruption of loving relationships. Families, communities, and nations are subject to dangerous actions committed by "angry" people. Solutions to these larger problems will only become possible when there develops in world consciousness a clear understanding of the relationship of anger to shame. Healthy modulation of worldwide anger is unattainable until those who feel weak, incompetent, disrespected, helpless, frustrated, disappointed, abandoned, rejected, isolated, lonely, and discriminated against have a voice that is heard and respected.

CHAPTER 8

WHEN RELATIONSHIPS GO BAD: COMPASS OF SHAME SPIRALS

Once upon a time, in a galaxy far, far away, a lovely princess fell in love with a handsome prince. Their love was so great that they remained interested in each other for an untold number of years, enjoying and discovering novelty in every moment of their time together. Their connection was so powerful that nothing interfered with or impeded it, ever. They never experienced feelings of rejection or hurt one another, ever. Never did they have to worry about or pay attention to shame in their relationship. They lived happily ever after.

Returning now to reality, our love relationships follow this same path but seldom for longer than a few weeks or months. Then, unlike our galactic prince and princess, the novelty begins to wear off. Perhaps it is the curse of having the most complexly evolved brain of any species ever discovered, but nothing remains novel to us forever. (Did I forget to mention that the prince and princess were microorganisms no bigger than amoebas?) All of our love relationships must contend with the fact that, by definition, **if the relationship is successful, novelty must diminish**. Early on, our emotional connection to one another is easily maintained because it is fueled by the natural interest and enjoyment generated by the fresh energy of newness. Remaining emotionally connected after the novelty wears off is complicated and the major challenge to the art of intimacy. It depends not on whether we are from Venus or Mars—or even California—but on how we handle the inevitable complications which appear and produce impediments to emotional connection. This is true for every human couple that has ever been in a committed, long-term relationship, regardless of sex. (Did I forget to mention that the prince and princess both had dual, interchangeable sex organs?)

How often have you heard someone say, "After we got married, his [or her] true nature came out"? Is this true? Are we really different after we make a long-term commitment and settle in together? I believe the answer is yes and no. "No" because it **is** part of our "true nature" to feel powerful interest in another person, especially when that person is new to us, and we experience that ineffable thing known as "chemistry" for one another. The intensity of initial interest-excitement in the other makes it easy for us to let down our guard and open up more of our inmost selves than we normally would. It is almost as if we revert to being childlike, relishing the back and forth sharing of interest with caregivers, and trusting—at least at first—that the other will not hurt us. As a result, rather than hide behind defenses that cover up our vulnerable self, we open up so our new love can know us deeply and completely. We want no impediments in the way of such a positive emotional connection.

The problem—the "yes" answer to the last question—arrives as the novelty begins to wear off and slowly but surely, our guard goes back up again. That guard is a learned component of all personalities, there to protect us against being hurt. It is as much a natural part of our learning as is learning the ABC's or 1 + 1 = 2. No childhood is devoid of experiences of shame, fear, or distress. People who do not learn to protect themselves from those feelings are in serious trouble. They are unable to minimize negative affect in interpersonal situations. Therefore, it is a *healthy* part of our makeup to be able to withhold parts of ourselves from others who might cause us harm, whether they do so wittingly or unwittingly. Normal growth and individuation produces people who can leave the protective environment of their families, go out into the world on their own, and defend themselves from the whims of others. Part of that process is developing the ability to hold ourselves in check and be guarded around others if need be.

As detailed in Chapter 6, the ways that people guard against shame include behaviors on the four poles of the Compass of Shame: attack other, attack self, withdrawal (hide from other), and avoidance (hide from self). These same defenses make an appearance in every relationship as novelty wanes, as impediments to emotional connection happen more often, and as shame is triggered more frequently. This is why people begin to experience the "other" side of their partner's "true nature." This side of a person can be extremely vulnerable to shame, depending upon a number of factors, including how caregivers attended to our most basic needs (see Chapter 3). One is usually less shame sensitive, and therefore less in need of powerful defenses, if raised by caregivers who connected well emotionally to them and whose child-rearing tactics did not include heavy-handed shaming. When the opposite has occurred, one can be extraordinarily sensitive to shame. For such people it is likely that whenever shame is triggered, the intensity of the attack other, attack self, withdrawal, or avoidance defense will be extreme. Such people are more "guarded" and less available emotionally. As mentioned earlier, all of us are vulnerable to shame, need at times to defend against it, and, therefore, routinely exhibit some degree of Compass of Shame defensive behaviors.

Let us now turn to a consideration of what happens when, as they inevitably will, things go wrong in a relationship and shame is triggered by impediments to emotional connection. It is important to keep in mind that we feel shame whether those impediments come from the natural evolution of the relationship or outside forces that are beyond our control. (A brief reminder: Our adult experience of shame usually registers in us as feelings of rejection, hurt, isolation, and a sense of distance from the other.) The degree of difficulty a couple encounters in these negative situations depends on how difficult the situation is, and how much shame sensitivity and defensiveness is present in each person. I will first outline the general principles involved in what I call Compass of Shame Spirals and then provide some examples of how relationships spiral in shame-based negative directions and present the greatest challenge to intimacy.

Compass of Shame Spirals

General principle: When an impediment to emotional connection creates shame in a relationship, *and the couple cannot use that information to make things better*, each will fall back on how they learned to defend against the insecure feelings generated by shame. Once activated, these shame defenses act as further impediments to emotional connection, which triggers more shame, then more defenses, then more shame, then more defenses, and so on. The most common result of this process is that couples repeatedly have the same "fights" without ever resolving them. At their worst, the cycles spiral downward into a place so negative that the only way to end the emotional pain is to lose interest in being in the relationship.

Compass of Shame spirals begin when one person in the midst of a shame reaction defends it with attack other, attack self, withdrawal, or avoidance. From there the spiral can take a number of different paths depending on how that person's partner defends against her or his shame. Compass of Shame spirals often occur in brief exchanges between partners. I think of these as "mini" spirals that are not necessarily significant or a bad omen for the relationship. They can usually be resolved without much difficulty. On the other hand, there are Compass of Shame spirals that are ruinous because they weave their way into the entire fabric of the relationship, becoming permanently scripted patterns of relating. These spirals happen because one, the other, or both partners carry deep-seated shame vulnerability from childhood issues and react to shame triggers with intense defensiveness.

The imaginary dialogue that follows is an example of a mini spiral. I created it from my experience listening to thousands like it in my office (and some in my own home). This dialogue relates to the scenario mentioned in an earlier chapter in which someone comes home excited about a recent happening only to be "shushed" by a partner engrossed in a TV show. I will present the dialogue first and then explain how it becomes a Compass of Shame spiral.

The scene opens with Mary sitting on the couch in the living room entranced by a PBS special about America's national parks. When she was a child, her family visited many of these parks. She was fascinated by them and during college returned often, spending days hiking and camping amid their beauty. Her large HDTV picture displays the stunning camera work in vivid detail. She is deeply absorbed in the historical narrative about the founding of the parks, much of which is new to her, when Marvin enters the room looking flushed and excited. He is just returning from playing in a golf tournament for the benefit of Susan G. Komen for the Cure, an international organization that has raised over a billion dollars in support of breast cancer research. On his last golf hole, there was a hole-in-one contest. Anyone who donated $100 to the charity and made a hole in one would win a brand-new $85,000 automobile. (The odds of an amateur golfer making a hole in one have been estimated as between 12,000 and 45,000 to 1.) Miraculously, Marvin made a hole in one—his first ever—and, in honor of his mother and sister, who both died of breast cancer, promptly donated the car to the charity. As he enters the house, he sees Mary watching TV, but he cannot contain himself:

Marvin: (excitedly) "The most incredible thing just happened!"

Mary: (not taking her eyes off the TV) "Shush, I'm really into this show."

Marvin: (hesitates, then angrily) "You always watch stupid shows like that."

Mary: (complete silence)

Marvin: (more angrily) "That's right, just sit there and ignore me."

Mary: (still not looking at him and now angry) "Oh, shut up! Why don't you go turn on that stupid computer of yours? You look at it more than I watch TV."

Marvin: (quieter but still with intensity) "What I do at the computer is important. What's so important about that TV show?"

Mary: (silence)

Marvin: (leaves in silence to turn on his computer)

Even though this is a fictional interaction, it highlights a circumstance that occurs frequently in all relationships—both people are highly interested in or excited about something in which the other does not have an immediate interest. It is very likely that when her TV show is over, Mary will be interested in Marvin's story. However, her stronger immediate interest in the show acted as an impediment to Marvin's interest in sharing when he came home. It is also reasonable to assume that later on Marvin will be interested in sharing Mary's excitement at seeing many of the places she visited in her younger days. However, the intensity of his excitement of the moment compelled him to want to share his feelings immediately, causing an interruption to her show, an interruption that acted an impediment to her interest and triggered shame in her. The result was an awkward situation that is not really anyone's "fault." Nonetheless, it created an emotional disconnection. Marvin experienced it as rejection and Mary experienced it as annoyance at first and then as hurt feelings.

Here is the dialogue again with a description of how the shame triggered by each step in the interaction set off a defensive Compass of Shame reaction, triggering more shame, then more defense, then more shame, then more defense as the spiral was set in motion. The emotions of this situation began with two people who love one another but who are both temporarily so interested in something else they are not able to focus on and connect with each other.

Marvin: (excitedly) "The most incredible thing just happened!"

Step 1: Marvin has great interest in sharing with Mary but it causes him to ignore how engrossed she is in her program.

Mary: (not taking her eyes off the TV) "Shush, I'm really into this show."

Step 2: Marvin's interruption impedes Mary's interest in the program. Her mild shame reaction is experienced as frustration that is quickly defended by a mild *attack other* with the "shush" followed by *withdrawal* back into the show.

Marvin: (hesitates, then angrily) "You always watch stupid shows like that."

Step 3: Mary's attack and withdrawal impede Marvin's interest in Mary being interested in him. His shame reaction feels like rejection, which he defends by an angry *attack other.*

Mary: (complete silence)

Step 4: Mary feels shame and hurt by his accusation that what she likes to watch on TV is "stupid." She defends her shame by further *withdrawal.*

Marvin: (more angrily) "That's right, just sit there and ignore me."

Step 5: Marvin now feels more intense shame and rejection because of her further withdrawal, and perhaps because he realizes he has been mean to her with his attack and use of the word *stupid.* He defends this shame with another round of *attack other.*

Mary: (still not looking at him and now angry) "Oh, shut up! Why don't you go turn on that stupid computer of yours? You look at it more than I watch TV."

Step 6: Her shame and hurt feelings intensify due to his latest attack. She, therefore, shifts her defense to the more intense, angry *attack other* mode.

Marvin: (quieter but still with intensity) "What I do at the computer is important. What's so important about that TV show?"

Step 7: Her angry attack notifies him that he went too far with his prior attack. He feels appropriately ashamed of what he said to her. Since he is still experiencing shame, he is not yet able to drop his defenses. However, he shifts modes of defense to **avoidance** with a rationalization about the relative importance of his work at the computer. He then offers up one more **attack other** by implying that her TV show is unimportant.

Mary: (silence)

Marvin: (leaves in silence to turn on his computer)

Step 8: Because things are unresolved, they remain emotionally disconnected, experiencing shame feelings triggered by disconnection. They simultaneously settle on **withdrawal** as a final defense in this sequence. Since continuing in Compass of Shame spirals is fruitless, the decision to be apart for a few minutes is a good one—the reasons for which I discuss in Chapter 10.

If a couple has the foundation for a good relationship and are able to be emotionally connected most of the time, then mini spirals like the one between Mary and Marvin work themselves out. Usually the bad feelings created by the spiral go away without any leftover resentment. Furthermore, healthy couples learn to use the message from moments of shame and develop ways to avoid future interactions of this nature as they develop skills for the practice of their art of intimacy.

Mary and Marvin's mini spiral raises several points of importance about Compass of Shame spirals. First, it is a serious misunderstanding of the basics of human relationships to see this interaction as simply being about anger—a mistake that virtually all fields of psychology have been making since the time of Freud. Of course, Mary and Marvin felt anger during this exchange, especially when engaged in attack other. However, their anger is a cover-up, a defense against more vulnerable feelings.

Secondly, Compass of Shame spirals have as their root cause *impediment to the basic need in both people to feel their partner's reciprocated interest*—i.e., he is interested in me and interested in me being interested in him, and vice versa. It is by shared interest that we keep emotional connection and intimacy alive. Moreover, it is through shared interest in an emotional connection that we feel loved and lovable, desirable, competent, and sexually attractive, and that we are capable of loving others. For better or worse, it is shame—and its oft-hidden challenge—that mediates this process, not anger.

Finally, all couples, married or unmarried, gay, lesbian, or heterosexual, will occasionally engage in Compass of Shame spirals, the vast majority of which are short-lived and end quickly with no real harm done.

It is a completely different story when Compass of Shame spirals originate from more deeply entrenched shame defenses. All of us have experienced plenty of shame long before our significant other ever put a smile on our face. As a result, we have all used every Compass of Shame defense at some time or another. If as children and adolescents shame has not overwhelmed us, then our defenses against it will be moderately flexible. The greater our flexibility, the more likely negative interactions with our partner will not only be resolved but will also be used as learning experiences enhancing the art of our intimacy.

For those in whom childhood experiences of shame were intense and unremitting, emotional survival required the development of more rigid defenses. In that case, either singly or in combination, attack other, attack self, withdrawal, or avoidance styles of handling shame dominate the personality. (It is beyond the scope of this book to detail why people develop different styles of handling shame. Suffice it to say, there is a complex mixture of societal, cultural, familial, and biological factors involved.) When shame defenses dominate a personality, that person's ability to remain emotionally connected is fragile at best. In addition, their partners experience great difficulty connecting to them through the entrenched defenses.

Compass of Shame Styles

Withdrawal/Attack Self married to Avoidance/Attack Other

An example of combined defenses, common in Western cultures, is when the physically stronger, allegedly more logical and independent male develops a style that is a mixture of avoidance and attack other, while the physically weaker, allegedly more emotional and dependent female develops a style that is a mixture of withdrawal and attack self. In the Compass of Shame diagram, one might place them as Man: A-AO and Woman: W-AS.

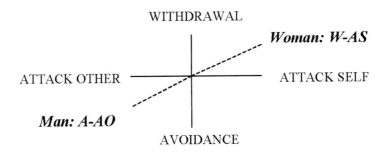

An extreme example of this combination is the macho man who can never admit he is wrong about anything (avoidance) and is exceedingly critical of his partner (attack other) whenever she makes the slightest mistake. His woman is often a shy, retiring (withdrawal), dependent person with exceedingly low self-esteem, who believes his criticism of her to be justified (attack self). Relationships between two people with shame defenses this rigid are seldom happy. There is little emotional connection possible. Both people are so heavily defended they cannot let anyone get close to them. The result is an endless, self-perpetuating Compass of Shame spiral with chronic intensification of shame in both people and, especially if drugs and alcohol are involved, physical violence frequently occurs. True emotional intimacy is rare in such couples.

To many of us, the surprising thing is that such people stay together, particularly when physical abuse is involved. Although an oversimplification—each case should be considered on its own—the women stay because their unresolved shame issues cause them to believe that no one else would ever want them and that they are too incompetent to make it on their own. The men stay because their unresolved shame issues induce in them the need to be in control and dominant, and they have found the perfect woman for that. These men cannot tolerate women who are forceful and have "a mind of their own."

There are several variations of Compass of Shame spirals. Which one becomes the common pattern for a couple evolves from an interaction between the shame defense most commonly employed by each partner. For instance, relationships can form between two people who both use withdrawal or where one uses withdrawal and the other avoidance or where both use avoidance or, the most contentious of all, where both use attack other as their primary shame defense. What follows are brief sketches of the kinds of emotional connection problems that arise when one, the other, or both partners are rigidly entrenched in shame defenses.

Withdrawal married to Avoidance

Sally and Ben met in graduate school while getting advanced degrees in architecture. They are both attractive, intelligent people who grew up in middle- to upper-middle-class families, and who have careers that are, for the most part, rewarding. They experienced a courtship filled with interest-excitement and enjoyment-joy. They fell in love, married, and had three children. From early on, however, Sally felt there was a problem with emotional connection, but their predominant defensive styles—*withdrawal* in her, *avoidance* in him—prevented them from being able to confront it.

While Sally noticed Ben often did not pay attention to her, she was hesitant to make her dissatisfaction known. For instance, during one of her pregnancies, they were in the city visiting friends. It was a cold winter night, and because parking near their friend's house was difficult, they had to leave their car many blocks away. After dinner, as they returned to the car, Ben ran far ahead and Sally, unable to keep up with him because of the pregnancy, lost sight of him. She felt abandoned and afraid. She mentioned something about it once she reached the car. When Ben ignored her with a brisk "I was freezing, so I was just trying to get to the car to warm it up," she said no more, even though she felt rejected both when he left her behind and when he did not seem to care how she felt about it.

While this story was a dramatic example of how Sally felt—and she recounted it in therapy even though it had occurred years before—there were many other, smaller things that bothered her. Ben would often sit on the couch after work wearing headphones and listening to his music, despite the fact that they had not seen each other for hours. He also had a tendency to disagree with any point of view she—or, for that matter, almost anyone else—expressed, using elaborately crafted lines of reasoning to prove he was right and they were wrong.

As the years went by, Sally withdrew more and more while Ben continued to think things were OK between them. The denial and hiding from his feelings through avoidance techniques never let him grasp the real situation. True, their once active sexual relationship had dwindled to almost nothing, but they did not fight, and Ben rationalized away the diminished sexuality as something that happens to all married people with children. He felt sexually attracted to other women and flirted verbally with one in particular, but it never went any further than talk. He was content with his "happy," healthy family, his career, his interest in his friends, sports, and his hobby flying model airplanes.

In fairness, he was not completely oblivious to Sally's occasional unhappiness. However, on those few occasions when he did happen to notice she was unhappy and ask her about it, he received little or no response from her. This led him to believe that she was not overly upset about whatever was making her unhappy, especially since, because of her withdrawal, he heard nothing else from her about it. However, one day about ten years into the marriage, she announced suddenly that she was leaving him because she had fallen in love with someone else. The man was a builder they had used for an addition to their house. At the time of her shocking announcement, she informed Ben that she and her lover were so serious that they had already finalized the plans for their dream house.

Ben was slam-dunked out of his denial. Initially, he experienced massive feelings of shame and rejection. This evolved briefly into shame rage at her and intense attack other. However, the attack other was short-lived because, as his mind raced back and forth reviewing his feelings for her, even back to when they met in college, he realized he loved her in spite of the affair. Moreover, he began to review his treatment of her and got in touch with his failure to be a good friend, ally, and lover. He convinced her to try couples therapy with him. She agreed but was skeptical that it would help.

In the initial therapy sessions, all of Ben's avoidance behavior disappeared. He was extraordinarily open about his failures and completely understood why Sally would have sought someone else to have her emotional needs met. He was so genuine in his remorse and in his expressions of love for her that she too began to open up and be more direct about her feelings. Several months into therapy, as her withdrawal lessened, she uncovered strong feelings for him she thought no longer existed. By dropping their usual defensive patterns, they rekindled the fire—the interest-excitement—in their relationship. She decided to stay with him, break up with the other man, and continue to work with Ben in therapy.

This particular Compass of Shame spiral developed as a response to impediments common to many marriages: career pressures, the joy and hard work of parenting, the mundane chores of daily life, and a slowly diminishing interest in sex. This couple hid the shame triggered by those impediments behind withdrawal (in her) and avoidance (in him). They did not fight or have horrible scenes filled with negative emotion. They just slowly spiraled apart, the shame defenses of each continuing to trigger more and more shame, and then more and more defensiveness until the shame from lack of emotional connection—with feelings of loneliness and isolation— led her into a new relationship.

Ben and Sally's case exemplifies how the combination of *avoidance* and *withdrawal* in the defensive styles of a couple is a mostly silent destroyer of relationships. There is not a lot of noisy yelling and screaming that would lead people to believe they had better do something fast to improve their relationship. Instead, the unrecognized shame slowly erodes the emotional connection and diminishes the strength of formerly positive feelings. In such situations, shame is truly hidden and a difficult challenge to continued intimacy.

Avoidance married to Avoidance or Withdrawal to Withdrawal

The same absence of strident confrontations is true for couples if both use avoidance or both use withdrawal as their defensive styles. These couples, when they do come into therapy, also report that they do not "fight" in the sense we usually think of, i.e., noisy yelling and screaming. One couple I worked with briefly years ago told me they had never raised their voices in twenty or so years of marriage. When I inquired as to why they sought couples therapy, they told me they did not feel very close and never did anything together. He was a professor of philosophy at a local university, and, while I cannot remember her profession, I do remember she was exceedingly bright also. They discussed the details of their lack of emotional connection, including at least a decade of no sexual relations, in a calm, considered, highly intellectual manner. As their opening remarks suggested, neither raised their voice, and both continually denied there were any "problems" or unresolved issues. They agreed that the lack of sex was a problem, but both intellectualized it away as being "normal" when you have children and get a little older.

I detected no signs that they actively disliked each other. They even smiled at one another a few times. When, shortly into the first session, they had nothing more to add, I asked if the absence of animosity between them was typical. They said yes. I pointed out that I noticed a few smiles and inquired if this was also typical. They said no, it was unusual for them to have such obviously positive feelings. In fact, they were a little surprised by them. They speculated that the positive feelings were a result of the discussion because it had been a long time since they had taken the time to discuss anything. This seemed a good sign and perhaps an indication that if they spent some time together, they might be able to rekindle more interest in one another. They agreed.

After a discussion of what they both enjoyed, they decided to go to lunch together. Promising to make a luncheon date as soon as they looked at their calendars, they scheduled an appointment with me for the following week and departed. My impression was that, although there had to be much more wrong between them than they were letting on, there was no way to access that information until they were more committed to the process of looking into their relationship. What was clear was how emotionless each was when they spoke about their relationship.

They returned the following week with the news that they had not been to lunch together, but they still thought it was a good idea. When asked why they had not been to lunch, they both agreed it had simply been a scheduling problem. The session was again devoid of much emotion as they discussed their marriage in a highly intellectualized fashion. Although a bit more of their history was uncovered, it remained free of any obvious reasons for their lack of interest in one another. They agreed they were in love when they married, but even though neither expressed feeling any animosity toward the other, neither professed feeling any love either. The session ended like the first: they were going to make a luncheon date and return the following week.

When they returned for the third session, they had yet to have a luncheon date. However, they informed me that they had discovered the problem. They were just not interested in one another anymore. Somewhere along the line, they had fallen out of love without so much as a whimper. They thanked me for helping them learn this lesson with clarity. They did not need to see me any longer because they had decided to part ways as soon as it became convenient for them to do so.

Their powerful intellectual styles and the shared Compass of Shame defense of avoidance had prevented them from recognizing the gradual diminution of their interest in one another. They had spiraled from a love relationship that mattered to both into a brother–sister, collegial relationship that was not very interesting. They did not even discuss their work because they were in different fields. Perhaps had they both been philosophers, a mutual interest in Socrates or Kant could have helped them remain emotionally connected or be more aware when they were not.

Attack Other married to Attack Other

Sometimes in the first minute of a session—even sooner when there are loud sounds emanating from my waiting room—I have no difficulty diagnosing relationships characterized by two people who are both stuck primarily in attack other. When I start the first session by asking such couples how I can help them, usually one or the other begins by detailing the myriad ways the partner has been mean, obnoxious, overly critical, untrustworthy, and otherwise impossible to live with. After I let that diatribe wind down, and because I have a permanent "equal time" provision in my office, I turn to the other and ask how I might help. I soon learn she or he will try to outdo the other with their laundry list of complaints. It is often the case that once they are finished venting, neither person has actually told me how I might help, or what they want from couples therapy.

On the surface, such couples act as if they only want a forum in which to complain about one another. Underneath those complaints is an obviously distressed relationship, two people who are severely emotionally disconnected. The good news about this combination of personality styles is that both people are well aware of and make known their feelings that something is dreadfully wrong. The bad news is that the attack other defense against shame is very resistant to change and doubly so when reinforced in a Compass of Shame spiral with a partner who uses the same defense.

The anger component in attack other—whether the form of expression is sarcasm, hostile criticism, or yelling and screaming—is a very effective defense against feelings of vulnerability and inferiority caused by shame. Among other things, anger can create a sense of "righteous indignation" in someone, causing them to believe deeply that they are "right" and the other is "wrong." It is worth noting that attack other arguments about who is right and who is wrong often alternate with the *avoidance* defense. This is because it is difficult for many to stay in an intensely angry state and continue attacking the other without experiencing some shame about the behavior. One can deny this shame and call up further anger if she or he can think of the next "logical reason" why the other is wrong or has wronged them and deserves to be attacked. However, in couples where both primarily defend shame with attack other, even allegedly "logical" arguments usually deteriorate into angry attacks.

Attack other behavior can be verbal or physical. One lesbian couple I worked with briefly consisted of a woman who weighed over 200 pounds and a woman who weighed less than 100 pounds. The smaller woman had, by her own admission, a "tongue like a knife." Her ability to rapid-fire intensely nasty remarks at her partner was remarkable. One day, her less mentally agile partner responded to a series of hostile comments by punching her senseless, and left her lying in the street outside of their house. This brought an end to the relationship and my unsuccessful attempts to help them.

Attack other behavior can be loud or quiet. A woman prone to loud, emotional complaints about her husband brought him into couples therapy, which he agreed they needed. After she voiced her complaints, he proceeded, in the quiet voice that both agreed he used all the time, to calmly describe her as overweight, illogical, just like her mother, and a "loser" when it came to her career choices. She became louder as she defended against his attack by accusing him of being so inattentive to their young children that she could not leave him alone with them. His even more quietly voiced retort was that since she had no friends, she never left the house anyway. At this point, I interceded and stopped the back-and-forth attack sequence. Fortunately, this couple, with help, could refocus and engage in a discussion of the positive aspects of their relationship, eventually leading to a commitment to couples therapy. Over time, they have significantly reduced their attack other behavior.

SUMMARY

The pattern of Compass of Shame spirals:

1) *Impediment to emotional connection* → Shame (rejection, isolation, distant, hurt feelings)

2) *Shame* → Compass of Shame defense (attack other, attack self, withdrawal, avoidance)

3) *Compass of Shame defense* → Impediment to emotional connection.

4) Return to number 1 and repeat.

CHAPTER 9

THE ART OF SHAME IN INTIMACY HOME REMEDIES: Part I

I f I have been successful to this point, it should be clear that shame is not an enemy—or at least does not have to be—but it does present a serious challenge to all intimacy. True, shame feels bad, and attempts to defend against it or make it go away can lead to problematic behaviors, some of which are potentially disastrous for relationships. But shame's inherited biological function—nature's wiring diagram in our brains—is to signal us when something we feel good about and want more of is withheld from us. In other words, *shame does not and cannot exist in the absence of positive feelings*. In this and the next chapter, I will describe how to put the natural function of shame to good use—how to use the information from shame to help you manage the feelings and emotions in relationships and sharpen your intimacy art. This information should be useful in all your relationships, but the focus of this book is committed peer relationships with a loved one.

Before I embark on a detailed journey through my "surefire" home remedies for relationship management, a very brief review of some salient points will help set the stage.

Chapter 2: Innate, inborn shame leads to an entire family of emotions. This family includes feeling ashamed, rejected, hurt, lonely, isolated, distanced, frustrated, exposed, disappointed, helpless, inferior, or disrespected.

Chapter 3: From childhood interactions, a pattern develops wherein we want to be together because we are interested in and enjoy others and have a strong interest in them being interested in and enjoying us. People help us feel better when we feel bad, triggering enjoyment in both of us.

Chapter 4: Emotional connection and intimacy emerge from our interest in and enjoyment of another and their interest in and enjoyment of us as we expose our inmost selves to one another.

Chapter 5: Impediments to emotional connection occur as a natural part of life. Impediments can come from intentional or unintentional behaviors and actions or from factors within or outside of the relationship. Impediments to emotional connection always trigger shame.

Chapter 6: Defenses against shame are necessary. They can make shame invisible—a challenge because the awareness of attack other, attack self, withdrawal, or avoidance types of behaviors or jealous and competitive feelings are useful messages that shame has been triggered.

Chapter 7: Anger is almost always a defensive reaction. It protects us from feeling completely helpless when something triggers our fear, distress, or shame. Expert analysis suggests that about 90% of the time we are angry, it is a defensive response to shame. One must look beneath anger to see the vulnerability in self and other.

Chapter 8: Shame defense in one partner is an impediment to emotional connection and triggers shame and shame defense in the other; this then acts as an impediment to emotional connection and triggers more shame and shame defense in the first partner and the cycle repeats.

Home Remedy Missions on the Path to Managing the Art of Intimacy

General Concepts

Yes, I believe relationships need "managing." They may come "naturally" at first, but in the real world, problems always arise. The question is how to deal with those problems effectively so they do not progress into regularly recurring nasty battles that gradually erode interest, enjoyment, and love. I base my approach on two relatively simple ideas—even though the theoretical underpinnings of those ideas are somewhat complex.

First, all of us enter into our most significant adult love relationship with inadequate knowledge and often distorted concepts of and capacity for emotional connectedness. In other words, we have a lot of emotional growing up to do, growth that can only take place in the context of a committed relationship where both partners seek intimacy.

Second, ***the content does not matter; how we feel about each other does.*** In other words, if we know how to make ourselves and our partners feel good about each other and our relationship, we can overcome and resolve even the most difficult of issues. I have worked with many couples whose relationships thrived after one of the partners had an affair because once the immediate crisis was over, they figured out how to feel good about one another and make the changes necessary to remain emotionally connected a much higher percentage of the time. I have also worked with couples who were seldom emotionally connected, who could not resolve even the simplest of issues—like who was "right" about where to squeeze the toothpaste tube—and who had to end the relationship because of seemingly trivial differences.

The general theoretical direction from which all of my suggestions for managing your emotional connection originate comes from my collaboration in the 1980s with Silvan Tomkins, the originator of affect psychology. His research revealed the Central Blueprint mentioned in Chapter 3. This is the general motivational program that develops in the brain and directs our behavior. One way of thinking about our "feelings blueprint" is to compare it to the blueprint a builder uses. He cannot take any action until he has a blueprint. He doesn't even know what size or shape to make the foundation until he sees that plan. Think of it this way: If you want to remodel your kitchen, you create some plan or blueprint ahead of time. You need to know where you want the sink, the stove, the oven, the fridge, the table and chairs before you start tearing things apart. Otherwise, your kitchen could end up utterly nonfunctional.

The central blueprint of motivation does this without our having to think about it. Because it is always at work, everything that happens to us is automatically analyzed using memory, and in the context that we experience positive affect as rewarding and negative affect as punishing. In healthy, emotionally intimate relationships where one sees the effective management of the emotional connection, each individual's blueprint is coordinated with their partner's blueprint—a process I call mutualization—to produce a balanced pattern of these four rules:

1)   The couple mutualizes and maximizes positive feelings;

2)   they mutualize and minimize negative feelings;

3)   they mutualize and minimize inhibiting the communication of feelings; and

4)   they mutualize and maximize the development of techniques to carry out 1–3.

Because our brain never stops following the four rules of this blueprint, it serves us well both as individuals and as couples to be aware that it is *the* motivational basis of all of our behaviors. Difficult circumstances may force the rules out of their natural tendency to remain in balance. When that happens, a person or couple may favor one strategy over another to the detriment of the relationship. For instance, when a couple cannot deal with negative feelings and reduce them effectively, they may choose an avoidance style and overly inhibit the expression and communication of feelings, while another couple in similar circumstances may seek nothing but positive feelings through the compulsive pursuit of excitement, perhaps with drugs, alcohol, heavy partying, affairs, etc. Such strategies seriously impede emotional connection. Couples who develop the relational skills to follow and balance the rules of the Central Blueprint are well equipped to handle life's inevitable impediments to emotional connection.

In my work with couples, I insist each person follow one general rule. It is worth keeping in mind while you digest the missions I propose for managing emotional connection. Tongue in cheek, and yet with great seriousness, I call it **Kelly's Rule Number One:**

If I do not have two people each taking care of themselves first, I have nothing to work with.

By taking care of yourself and refusing to be abused verbally or physically, by knowing what you need to maximize your own positive feelings and minimize your own negative feelings, by caring for your body, your mind, and your spirit, you also take care of your relationship. I liken this to the announcement by flight attendants at the beginning of each flight: "If air pressure in the cabin drops and the oxygen masks deploy and you are traveling with small children, place your own oxygen mask on first." This is excellent advice for the general management of one's emotional life. It does those around you little good if you perish from lack of oxygen or lack of proper care of the self.

People who are unable to care for themselves have poor relationships and poor capacity for managing emotional connection, and often need individual therapy before they can make use of couples therapy or the suggestions in this book. (It is my bias, however, that personal growth is never complete until done with one's partner in the context of a loving relationship.) If you do feel that you can take care of yourself, then what follows are a series of missions—presented more or less in the order in which they need doing—whose successful completion will help you and your partner fully develop your art of intimacy. One caveat: None of us should ever be content that we have fully completed any of these missions. It is best to think of them as ongoing missions with goals that we continually strive to meet, redoubling our efforts whenever things start going downhill in our relationship.

Mission 1: Maximize Awareness of Feelings in the Self

Throughout this book, and especially in "A Primer of Affect Psychology" found in Appendix I, I have outlined the fundamentals of the biological basis of human motivation. The important point again is this: our affect system is an information-gathering mechanism that allows us to be consciously aware of what is going on around and inside of us. We become conscious of something when and only when one of the nine innate affects is triggered. (Reminder: Once we become aware of an affect, we call it a feeling.) In other words, feelings (affects) moderate our conscious awareness of the world around us. (How we interpret that awareness evolves from a combination of our feelings, our past memories, learning, and the cognitive functions of our brain.) There is never a conscious waking moment when we do not have feelings, even if we are unaware of them. Lack of awareness of our feelings occurs either because we have been taught not to pay attention to them or because the intensity level of a particular feeling is so low, we do not notice it.

The truth of the matter is that to "manage" any aspect of our lives efficiently, we must be aware of what motivates us. Since we must be aware of our feelings to know what motivates us, then it follows that *to know how to manage our relationships, we must be aware of our feelings.* As mentioned before, Western culture is generally afraid of feelings. Because young children cannot modulate their feelings and usually express fear or distress or anger or excitement or joy in "loud" vocalizations or behaviors, there is a strong cultural bias forcing caregivers to "quiet" their children to make them socially acceptable. Parents experience shame if their children do not act in public the way that society expects they should.

Individual families vary in how they accomplish this "socialization." Some use mostly fear, some mostly anger, and some mostly shame, but generally, caregivers use varying combinations of these feelings to quiet their children. To complicate matters further, there are often significant differences in the way families socialize boys and girls. Generally, a girl is more likely to be shamed for noises or behaviors deemed inappropriate in her culture; while boys are more likely to be subjected to techniques that utilize fear and anger—techniques that also create shame because they make the boys feel small, inferior, and helpless. And I shudder to think about how often in North American cultures, when a little boy cries or acts afraid, he is shamed by the words "Act like a man!" Or when a little girl gets upset, she is told she is being "too emotional."

We all carry far too much shame about expressing feelings to others because of socialization. We get embarrassed about crying in public or even in front of close friends. We often suppress our anger at some offense against us, only to think later about what we should have said and how angry we should have been. Stated another way, the process of socialization creates patterns in most of us whereby we consciously withhold our feelings. The more we have to withhold feelings from others, the more we become unaware of them ourselves. The more we become unaware of our feelings, the more we lose the ability to track changes in our feelings, especially the nuances of small changes. This is a significant problem for relationships because feelings and changes in feelings give us important information about our emotional connection.

Lack of awareness of feelings is not just a problem for relationships. It is also a serious problem for knowing and being aware of the self. Feelings (affects) make us aware of both our inner and outer worlds, and motivate us from birth on. Feelings are an integral part of memory and how memory is stored. Feelings are also an integral part of personality and how personality develops. As a result, feelings are vital to who we are. To be unaware of our feelings robs us of the ability to know ourselves intimately. If we cannot know our self, then we cannot open our self to an intimate other … nor can we take care of our self properly—a clear violation of Kelly's Rule Number One.

Therefore, your first mission—hopefully not mission impossible—is a difficult one for many people: **you need to assess your level of awareness of your feelings.** Do you always know what you are feeling? Do you only know what you are feeling when the feelings are strong? Can you distinguish between different feelings?

Here is a quick exercise, but one you might consider doing multiple times each day. From the list below, identify what you are feeling **right now**. (Here is a crib sheet with pictures to help remind you of the nine basic affects outlined in Appendix I, and to remind you that the face is a valuable key to recognizing feelings.)

INTEREST	ENJOYMENT	STARTLE

FEAR	DISTRESS	ANGER
	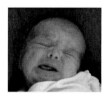	

DISGUST	DISSMELL	SHAME

I hope you decided you felt *interest* in the exercise. But if, while reading, your mind wandered to some problem or another in your life, you might have discovered that you felt *distress* or *fear* or *shame* about that problem. Whatever you were feeling, it had to originate in one of these nine basic affects. They are the building blocks, transcribed by evolution into our genetic code, for all feelings and emotions.

There is yet another problem in identifying what we feel. As described earlier, **emotions** are the result of lifelong learning from observations of how others respond to our basic affects and how those others appear to us when they have any of those affects. The nine building blocks of affect form the foundation for a huge variety of emotions. I have seen word lists of "emotions" (sometimes mislabeled as feelings) with hundreds of entries. Such lists cause much more confusion than clarity. For instance, it is often the case that two people use the same "emotion" word to describe what they are feeling. This tricks them into believing that they are "feeling" the same thing, when in actuality each feels something quite different.

To help you identify what you are feeling, I suggest that you stick to the list of the nine innate affects (feelings). One of the major advantages of doing so is that while we may all appear different "emotionally," we all have the same nine basic feelings. Every man and woman alive **knows** what it is to feel *fear, interest, distress, enjoyment, anger, shame, disgust, and dissmell,* and to be *startled.* In this respect, we are all much more alike than we are different. Books, theories, and therapies about improving relationships that ignore these similarities are all doomed to failure. We need, of course, to have an intellectual understanding of our differences. But the knowledge, for instance, that my wife is more "right"-brained and I am more "left"-brained doesn't matter one little bit when we are having an argument. If you really want to achieve empathic attunement with your partner, to know and share in what he or she is going through, then find out what he or she is feeling and compare it with your experience of that same feeling. The ability to be emotionally connected and practice the art of intimacy to its fullest originates in feelings. To repair emotional disconnection, what matters most is how we feel.

Although I encourage awareness of feelings every minute of the day, I recognize that this is a difficult mission. It may help to reflect that, when you were a child, you did so without thinking. Look at your children or those of others. When you see a child's face, do you have any trouble recognizing what she or he is feeling? No; children do not disguise their feelings the same way adults do. Their fear or shame or interest or distress or enjoyment is written all over their faces. As adults, we still have that in us if we can overcome the forces of socialization imposed by our families and our communities. Overcoming those forces requires us to be vigilant of our fear and shame about letting others see what we feel. But "no worries," as my Australian friends say. As adults, we have much more control over and ability to modulate our feelings than we did as children. So whatever feelings you allow to surface and be visible on your face will probably not scare your partner. Instead, a partner who is really interested in you will be grateful to be included in your emotional world, will feel more fully connected with you, and will be more than willing to join you in the mission of overcoming old scripts that block the expression of feelings.

After I teach my patients about the nine basic affects or feelings, there is a game I suggest to help them with the mission of being aware of feelings at all times. I have them imagine that each time their phone rings, it might be me or the "feelings police" calling. (This is an even better game since the invention of cell phones.) They should be prepared to answer the question "What are you feeling right now?" without hesitation. It takes only a few seconds with each ringtone to play this game as a reminder to tune into one's feeling state.

If someone is momentarily stuck deciding which of the nine feelings is present, I suggest they simplify the task by deciding whether it feels more like a positive or more like a negative feeling. In other words, does it feel like you want more of whatever you are feeling or that you want the feeling to stop? Once you make that decision, things become a little easier. If, for instance, it is a positive feeling, then it is either interest-excitement or enjoyment-joy or a mixture of these two good feeling affects. It is often more difficult for people to decide exactly which negative feeling is present. Anger, disgust, and dissmell are fairly easy to distinguish from one another. The commonly used word *anxiety*, however, can cause a great deal of confusion when it comes to deciding if one is feeling fear, distress, or shame.

My study of how people use "anxiety" has turned up at least four possible meanings. It can mean the person feels fear (I'm anxious about walking down that dark alley), feels distress (I'm anxious about all the work I have to do), feels fear of shame (I'm anxious about that speech I have to give), or is highly interested in something (I'm anxious to get to the golf course). And *anxiety* is not the only word that complicates our ability to be specific about what we feel. For example, when asked what they feel, many people experiencing negative feelings respond with "I'm confused." This is a phrase that is better suited to a description of mixed-up thoughts than to feelings. It would take far too many pages to go into a lengthy description of all the words muddling our ability to be aware of and describe what we feel. I mention only these two to draw attention to the problems people face when they try to become more aware of specific feelings, especially the difficulty some have in deciding whether they are feeling fear, distress, or shame. As a further aid in making that distinction, here is a brief description of the general sense of what each feels like (see Appendix I for a more detailed description of the affects):

Fear: a feeling that too much is happening too fast, too soon, and it is scary.

Distress: a feeling that too much is happening for too long and it feels like a heavy load.

Shame: feeling ashamed or any of the family of emotions listed in Chapter 2.

Mission 2: Trust What You Feel and Own It

I mean this when I say to you,
All feelings good and bad are true.[3]

The writer of these song lyrics echoes the findings of all the research based on affect psychology. If you feel something, then it is neither right nor wrong. It is simply a biologically based "statement of fact" from a message received in your brain about what is going on around and/or inside of you.

If someone tells you you are wrong about what you are feeling, do not believe them!

What motivates someone to tell you your feelings are wrong is their own discomfort, their negative affect that they want stopped. Even if this is someone who loves you, the problem created by their negating the validity of your feelings is that it impedes the emotional connection between the two of you, creating shame in you.

When you achieve some success carrying out Mission 1, an unshakable certainty about your feelings develops, regardless of the opinions of others—be they gently stated or in the form of bullying. Trust in your feelings is an invaluable tool for the successful practice of the art of intimacy. If another is made uncomfortable by your feelings and emotional disconnection occurs, your trust in yourself will reduce the intensity of the resulting shame, which will reduce the intensity of your defenses against that shame, which will increase the chances that you can reconnect sooner rather than later, which will decrease the chances of the two of you engaging in a Compass of Shame spiral. Here is an example of how this might work. It is a rather simple example, but it demonstrates the pattern I am suggesting you adopt in these situations.

"I'm afraid of that big dog."

"Don't be silly, there's nothing to be afraid of."

"No, I really am afraid because a dog just like that bit me once."

"Oh, I'm sorry. I didn't know that."

3. "These Ain't Tynan's Blues" by Danny Schmidt. Copyright © 2001 Live Once Records. All rights reserved. Used by permission.

"Can you help me with my fear?"

"Yes, I happen to know this dog very well. He is big, but friendly. You stand behind me while I call him over and pat him, and then, when you feel less afraid, you can pat him, too."

This pattern is useful in even the most difficult of situations. It **only** works if the first person trusts their feelings sufficiently to avoid defensive reactions when their partner negates those feelings. In the example, the fearful person clearly accepts their fear as real and not "silly," quickly bypasses any feelings of shame, and gives the other more information about the origin of the fear. This openness invites an emotional connection rather than impedes it. It encourages the other to connect with the feelings and be helpful. The experience becomes a shared one where the people feel like allies engaged in mutualizing and minimizing a negative feeling. Every incident like this that follows the central feelings blueprint—and it does not matter if it is large or small in the minds of those involved—enhances feelings of intimacy.

Being accurate in our interpretations about why we feel the way we do is not always as straightforward as in this example. While our central nervous system is biologically without bias—it simply responds with an affect to certain stimulus conditions—a lifetime of learning creates emotional responses that are completely biased. They are based, in part, on a complex system of beliefs passed down from generation to generation and unique to the particular cultural milieu in which they were learned. Such beliefs are usually quite rigid and stubbornly resist change or the input of new information.

A belief currently held by many in Western culture is that if you feel bad, it must be someone else's "fault." One of the origins of this belief is shame about feelings induced by the process of socialization discussed earlier. The result is that if you can blame someone else for how you feel, then you do not have to take responsibility for those feelings or have shame about them. While this may momentarily reduce your shame, blaming your significant other for how you feel is a form of attack other. It triggers shame and subsequently defense against shame in them. They may then attack you back or withdraw from you or deny they had anything to do with what you are feeling. As a result, you will both be engaged in defensive processes that impede emotional connection.

This very common cycle of shame-induced blame followed by defense followed by further blame and further defense is preventable—

and treatable. To prevent or interrupt it requires that both partners: 1) develop a clear awareness of what they are feeling, **and** 2) have a willingness to own that feeling. These are two of the major treatment goals of all professional couples therapists, even though they come from many different schools of thought and therapeutic systems. Whether the therapist is aware of it or not, achievement of these goals reduces shame and shaming in disturbed couples. **All effective therapies reduce shame**, in spite of what you may have seen or heard spouted by the many TV and radio therapist-performers whose main goal is to promote themselves and their shows.

Perhaps the most common therapeutic technique of real-life therapists is to help a couple alter their style of communication. For instance, a blaming statement (attack) heard frequently in the early stages of couples therapy goes something like:

"I feel that you never listen to anything I say!"

At first glance, it may appear that the speaker **is** talking about their feelings. However, no matter how accurate they may be in their description of the other's behavior, "You never listen to anything I say" is **not** a feeling. It exposes nothing about the innermost feelings of the speaker. It is a disguised attack guaranteed to create shame, followed by defensiveness in the partner. It is a sentence spoken by someone defending against their own shame. Furthermore, it does not invite any change in the situation, nor does it indicate any willingness on the part of the speaker to take responsibility for anything. Here is an alternative statement spoken by someone in the later stages of therapy. It encapsulates a more advanced awareness of feelings and a willingness to own one's feelings to promote emotional connection:

"I feel lonely when we can't talk. What can I do to make it easier for you to hear me?"

One could substitute any one of the shame family of emotion words—e.g., disappointed, rejected, hurt, distant, frustrated, or helpless—in place of the word lonely, but the use of *lonely* in this case conveys the greatest sense of vulnerability in the speaker. Vulnerable exposure of the self indicates a true interest in examining the problem and being more intimate. It invites the partner to act as if the two are allies rather than enemies. Such exposure is only possible if one can own their feelings and trust them.

Because the behaviors and emotions of others do impact us emotionally, it can be difficult to sort out and own our feelings. For instance, in the example above, whose "fault" is it that the refusal to listen by one partner (let's call him Jake) triggers shame in the other (Abby)? This is a trick question. If one thinks in terms of fault, then someone must always be to blame. If you must blame someone for how you feel, then you will be unable to own your feelings, and you will be the cause of impediment to emotional connection. In this situation, Abby feels shame (lonely feelings) when Jake's refusal to listen impedes her interest in him and in her interest in him hearing what she has to say. It sounds confusing, but all it really means is that if Abby had no interest in having a relationship with Jake, then she would not care—would not have shame triggered—that he does not listen.

Through therapy, Abby and Jake learned that shame is triggered only if positive feelings already exist. Because Abby was very willing to own her feelings, she accepted that her shame (lonely feelings) was a natural result of her love for (interest in) Jake. When she no longer needed to blame Jake for her feelings, she altered the way she spoke to him whenever she became aware of the presence of shame during interactions between them.

Because of her newly gained awareness of her feelings, her trust in her feelings, and her willingness to own them, instead of an attack, Abby exposes her feelings by saying, "I feel lonely when we can't talk." Then she expresses an interest in Jake by inviting him to explore with her what she might do differently to help him connect with her: "What can I do to make it easier for you to hear me?" In this statement, she blames neither herself nor him for the problem. (The real situation between such folks is, of course, more complicated. For purposes of simplification, I avoided discussion of the sources of Jake's shame evidenced by his withdrawal and apparent refusal to listen.) The important point is that blame of self or other when shame feelings surface is an impediment to emotional connection and intimacy.

Here is another example of how to reduce blaming interactions by owning one's feelings. My lovely wife responds to negative messages from her feet at the end of the day by taking off her shoes wherever she happens to be when her feet begin to hurt. She often receives these messages while in a major corridor of the house. As a consequence, for years now, both in broad daylight and in the dark of night, I have tripped over shoes in the middle of our kitchen, the middle of our bedroom, or on the way to the master bathroom. My reaction when I unexpectedly encounter her shoes varies. Sometimes I mutter, "What the @#$%!" and kick the shoes out of the way. At other times, I calmly place the shoes to the side, chuckling to myself, "Yup, that's her all right."

The difference in my reaction clearly has nothing to do with her behavior and everything to do with my emotional state at the time. Each time I become annoyed at the situation, I am able to discern that I was already in distress when her shoes and I met. I could blame my annoyance on her. However, to do so would be to deny that my feelings just before I step on the shoes have anything to do with my reaction, when in fact, those feelings have *everything* to do with how I respond at the time. Once couples learn greater awareness of their feelings, they report a significant diminution of blaming interactions. To see affect in the self and own it often removes one of the most frequent impediments to emotional intimacy encountered in relationships. (And, to be completely fair, I must admit that I now seldom encounter my wife's shoes in unexpected places.)

Mission 3: Maximize Awareness of the Flow of Feelings in the Relationship

The reward for improving the awareness of your affect, trusting what you feel and owning it is that these actions give you invaluable information about the flow of emotions between you and your partner. There is full agreement in the extensive literature about relationships that we affect one another's emotions. Some experts focus more on here-and-now interpersonal interactions and others focus more on what we bring from childhood relationships to our current relationship, but most consider that what happens between partners is the result of both here-and-now events and how earlier learning influences our responses to those events.

In my opinion, we first have to learn in the here and now how to manage our relationship before we can help one another deal with influences from earlier learning. If we cannot effectively reduce negative feelings between us in our daily interactions, then shame will block our interest in mutual exploration of each other's past. Furthermore, we will be less likely to develop the sense of alliance, friendship, and trust in the relationship necessary before one is willing to carry out deeply personal explorations into the self in the company of another. Here, then, are a few thoughts about how to attend to the feelings and emotions we trigger in each other in the here and now.

Feelings between you and your partner ebb and flow from positive to negative with varying levels of intensity. (Some might argue that there are times when no feelings are present. I insist, based on the biology of affect, that such is not the case. The seemingly "no feelings" states occur because the feelings present are either of very low intensity or the people involved have learned to be unaware of them.) One of the primary means by which feelings emerge in our relationships is based on the phenomenon of **affect contagion**. This is a purely biological mechanism whereby an affect in one person triggers the same affect in another. A prime example of affect contagion is the experience of distress most of us have had when in the presence of a child crying in distress, especially if we are in a confined space such as the cabin of an airplane. Each affect (feeling) has a specific effect on us such that our face, body language, and speech all carry the traits of that affect (see Appendix I for a more detailed explanation). Therefore, we feel, without even thinking about it, what another is feeling as we resonate with their facial expression, body posture, and tone of voice. Whether we are aware of that feeling depends upon how attuned we are to our own feelings.

The better we know someone and the more time we spend with them, the more "expert" we become in that person's feelings. Hence, the mere raising of an eyebrow by our partner signifies much more to us than it would to a stranger. It can sometimes trigger powerful feelings and emotional responses in us. Here is the best way to think about feelings in your relationship:

When together, you are feeling something every minute, your partner is feeling something every minute, and these feelings influence the flow of the feelings between you every minute.

Obviously, if someone is more unaware than aware of their feelings, they will be poorly equipped to manage these feelings. However, even if you have the ability to recognize feelings with some accuracy, you still have a choice to make. You can use your awareness of feelings proactively to manage your emotional connection or you can let the feelings manage you—a clear violation of Kelly's Rule Number One.

If you set a goal to be as emotionally intimate and close to one another as you can be every minute of the day, this is where the information about shame and the defenses against shame will have the greatest value. **Every time shame is triggered in your relationship, something is impeding your desire to be emotionally connected**. To avoid the unpleasantness of Compass of Shame spirals, you must recognize the presence of shame and do something about it right there and then. If you do this, you will avoid the problems created by negative feelings that linger, create ongoing defensiveness, and make it impossible to feel close to one another.

There are many ways people can reconnect after moments of disconnection. Regardless of the suggestions I make to couples in therapy, they all end up finding their own unique ways of reconnecting, ways that fit their personalities and the distinctive nature of their relationship. In the next chapter, I will make a number of suggestions in that same spirit as I continue to offer "home remedy" missions. But I fully recognize and honor the fact that every couple practices the art of intimacy somewhat differently because nobody knows better than you and your significant other how to do what must be done to feel emotionally connected.

CHAPTER 10

THE ART OF SHAME IN INTIMACY HOME REMEDIES: Part II

Missions 1–3 in the previous chapter all derive from direct observations of *feelings*, both yours and your partner's. The next mission requires an analysis of *behaviors*, both yours and your partner's. This analysis is necessary because, due to the painful nature of shame, we usually convert most feelings of shame into behaviors that disguise it. Humans have the ability to become exceptionally skilled at many things that, when successful, become so automatic we do not even have to think about or be aware of their activation. This is especially true when it comes to our defenses against shame. As a result, we often do not recognize our feelings of shame. To be fully aware of when shame is triggered during an interaction between us and our significant other, we must scrutinize our behaviors and learn to uncover the feelings motivating them.

Mission 4: Maximize Awareness of Defenses Against Shame

Assuming that you have begun to work on Mission 3 from the last chapter, you will experience an increase in interest in what is happening in the emotional atmosphere between you and your partner. Since any break in your emotional connection triggers an immediate alarm in the brain, it does not matter if you are aware of it happening, you will still experience shame in the form of one of the shame family of emotions. You will briefly feel such things as hurt, lonely, rejected, isolated, or distant from your partner, but, in most circumstances, rapidly rid yourself of those shame feelings through a defensive response.

I described the defenses against shame in detail in Chapter 6, and perhaps you have already decided which are the usual, automatic defensive responses employed by you and your partner. I present them again here in order to provide you with some techniques to: 1) interrupt such defensiveness, and 2) convert the information provided by shame defenses into behaviors beneficial to intimacy. It is essential to make some changes in your characteristic way of defending against shame; otherwise, you will be party to Compass of Shame spirals that create impediments to intimacy.

It is critically important to understand that the successful letting go of a shame defense will make you feel more vulnerable.

This is both good news and bad news. The good news: Being more vulnerable allows both partners freer, less impeded access to their inmost selves, and to the inmost self of the other. Such access is vital to the refinement of our ability to follow the Central Blueprint, maximize our emotional connection, and increase our skills in the art of intimacy.

The bad news: Being more vulnerable allows both partners freer, less impeded access to their inmost selves and the inmost self of the other. Any time we open ourselves up in this way, we become more vulnerable to being shamed. We have all experienced the paradox about loving someone:

You cannot emotionally connect freely without the risk of shame and hurt.

Since all of us began developing our shame defenses very early in life, they are old habits that are especially difficult to confront and break. You will need to enlist the help of your partner in this task. I suggest you inform your partner up front that you plan to try to be less defensive, more open and vulnerable. Share with her or him your fear that, if in your greater vulnerability, she or he does something that triggers shame, you will backslide by resorting to more of the old defense. Please remember also to be kind to yourself when you do discover moments of the old defensiveness. Old habits do not die easily. Nor do they die in a linear fashion. Successful change always proceeds in fits and starts until both partners become comfortable with the new way of relating. So anticipate ups and downs in this process.

Here are a few questions you might ask yourself to help you determine your characteristic defense against shame:

For *attack other*:
Do I often get angry with my partner for no apparent reason?
Do I angrily accuse her/him of being stupid, silly, incompetent, or unattractive?
Do I angrily blame her/him whenever something goes wrong in our relationship?
Do I often attack her/him with sarcasm?

For *withdrawal*:
Do I remain silent whenever we are having trouble?
Do I find myself avoiding her/him too much of the time?
Do I find myself disinterested in sex or turned off to her/him?
Do I resist sharing my real feelings with her/him?

For *avoidance*:
Do I think things are fine between us, but my partner never does?
Do I need to out-talk my partner to prove I am right?
Do I believe I am always right?
Do I often turn to alcohol or other drugs when things go wrong between us?
Do I get involved in affairs in spite of feeling that I still love her/him?

For *attack self*:
Do I always think I'm wrong or to blame, and she/he is right?
Do I feel like a bad person whenever she/he complains about something?
Do I feel like I'm stupid and she/he is smart?
Do I feel like hurting myself when things go wrong between us?

Everyone uses some degree of each of these defensive maneuvers from time to time. In general, while we may resort to a single defense from time to time, most of us end up utilizing combinations of the shame defenses. The most common combinations are *attack other* with *avoidance*, and *withdrawal* with *attack self*. In other words, someone who regularly attacks their partner with angry recriminations about what that person is doing wrong is almost always in complete denial, avoiding their part—their shame—in what goes wrong between them. On the other hand, the person who regularly withdraws when problems occur is usually someone who is very negative about the self, believing that they are the cause of most of what goes wrong because they are too stupid or ugly or unlovable.

With these ideas in mind, I suggest you spend some time analyzing your characteristic defenses against shame. Being clear that shame has been set in motion—and that there is, therefore, an active impediment to your emotional connection—is a prerequisite for doing something about it. It gets you ready for the next mission, which is somewhat more difficult.

Mission 5: Challenge Your Defenses Against Shame Openly with Your Partner

You will have no difficulty recognizing when you have successfully begun Mission 5. You will feel more vulnerable and exposed to your partner. The best way to start is to select a calm, emotionally connected moment with your partner, make it clear that what you are about to say is difficult for you because it will make you more vulnerable, and then plunge ahead with "I know I need to change [insert here one of the shame defenses] in order to make our relationship better."

It is extremely helpful if your partner collaborates in the work of changing your defensive style. Needless to say, it makes your mission easier if he or she can open up about their defensive style at the same time. However, if you find yourself refusing to change because your partner is not ready or is not "trying" also, then a reexamination of your motives is in order. The notion "I'm not going to try if she/he is not going to try" is another defense against shame and will only create more impediment to emotional connection and more shame. In addition, if neither partner is willing to risk "going first" in change-making, then nothing will change. Someone has to make the first move.

Sharing with your partner that you plan to stop attacking or withdrawing or avoiding when things go wrong is a good starting point. Please be advised, however, that you will only achieve success at change after many trials at dropping your defenses. After all, defenses against shame begin early in one's life and repeat many times over the years. They are difficult habits to break. Changes in habits only occur if you acknowledge to yourself and your partner that "I'm doing it again" each time you find the pattern repeating. If you do so regularly, you will begin to diffuse the shame reactions in each of you and lessen the chance that Compass of Shame spirals get set in motion. The interruption of these spirals makes it possible to initiate joint explorations into the actual causes of the shame. This is difficult at first because when shame is successfully hidden behind defenses, its causes are likewise hidden. However, you are now equipped with the following information:

Shame is a vital tool for making your relationship better, and

Shame is triggered by impediments to your emotional connection; therefore,

You are looking for an impediment blocking the *good feelings* about one another.

Joint interest in finding and removing impediments begins to make things better right away, because that action—shared interest—reconnects people. It makes them feel less isolated from one another and more like allies dealing with a mutual problem. This reduces shame and triggers feelings of joy and hope that you can deal with and overcome bad feelings in the future. In other words, once a couple tackles this task in earnest, they have begun utilizing the power of the Central Blueprint of motivation to enhance their emotional connection.

Mission 6: Follow the Central Blueprint with Your Partner

The Central Blueprint for motivation as described in Chapters 3 and 9 and in Appendix I is a set of rules linking our biology and our psychology. These rules motivate us automatically, usually without our paying much attention to them. The mission here is to make ourselves overtly conscious of the rules and use them proactively as best we can, as both individuals and couples.

One cannot just sit around passively waiting for these things to happen, especially as we all bring ready-made defenses against shame to our relationships. These defenses cause distortions of the rules and produce emotional imbalances in each individual, thus creating serious impediments to emotional connection.

The remainder of this chapter is devoted to suggestions about how to make conscious use of these rules in order to engage proactively in connecting better with your partner. The goal here is to enhance emotional balance because the better balanced we are emotionally, the easier and more rewarding it is to open up our inmost selves to our partner and feel emotionally connected. (Clear attention to the rules of the Central Blueprint is the key to following Kelly's Rule Number One.)

Mission 6a: Mutualize and Maximize Positive Feelings

If you have ever been in an exciting long-term love relationship, then you have experienced the decline in those early, very positive feelings as the novelty of the relationship wears off. It is not that your partner cannot still surprise you, because that happens in all relationships that are successful over long periods. Novelty declines by **natural** processes if a relationship is successful. I have worked with many couples who have gotten into difficulty simply due to their misunderstanding of the effects of the loss of novelty or their failure to do something to counteract it.

This is where the knowledge that it is *normal* for shame to be triggered can be vitally important. A couple, sensing any of the shame family of emotions, can use that message to understand clearly what is going wrong. One "symptom" of shame is a diminished frequency of sexual interactions. Over the years, I have been told by couples countless times that when they reengaged in sexual activity, they were amazed at how much closer they felt and how a number of little things they had been upset about now seemed very trivial.

One couple with a successful long-term marriage told me they always knew when it was time to go on vacation. If they found themselves sniping at one another over mostly insignificant things, they would plan a trip. The novelty of being in a new location almost always stirred them up sexually and they would come home significantly better connected than before. I believe that there is a great deal of evidence that in very many situations—in my mind, the majority—when things are going poorly for a couple, the problem is not so much the issues involved as the way the two people feel about one another. They can deal with issues effectively if they feel emotionally connected, and the opposite is painfully true.

Sex is an excellent means of rekindling interest-excitement and enjoyment-joy, but it is only one of many possible ways people can mutualize and maximize positive feelings. For the very busy married couple with children who do not go out very often together, I always recommend that they begin dating again. Sometimes a simple dinner out does wonders for emotional intimacy, if they can find a babysitter. Going to the movies, a weekend together at a nearby B&B, or anything else that is a shared interest will trigger novelty and hence more interest in one another.

A note about verbal communication for the mutualizing and maximizing of positive feelings: **It is important but not mandatory.** Some people, especially those who utilize the withdrawal defense against shame, cannot open up to their significant other verbally until the emotional connection between them improves. Having sex or going to the movies or taking a walk or just sitting on the living room couch together without talking may be necessary at times—the foreplay before verbal intercourse, if you will—before certain people can open up verbally.

Many have the mistaken idea that two people MUST talk before things can be better between them. This is nonsense and comes from a misunderstanding of what really motivates people to seek emotional connection with others. Forced talk can be too shaming for those who need withdrawal to feel safe[4] and/or those who lack verbal skills. The effect of making them talk before they are ready can be greater defensiveness. That said, once two people do feel emotionally connected, they can deepen that connection by verbally sharing all aspects of their inmost selves, including both their positive and negative feelings. Sharing negative feelings is ultimately critical because they are an inevitable part of all relationships. This brings us to the next mission, because how we share negative feelings so that they do not make things worse is often very tricky.

Mission 6b: Mutualize and Minimize Negative Feelings

If someone is experiencing negative emotion about their relationship, they are going to communicate that negativity in words, body language, and tone of voice. This will more than likely trigger negative emotions in their partner, escalating the bad feelings in the first person, and Compass of Shame spirals can be set in motion. My first suggestion to couples who consult me for couples therapy because of frequent serious fighting—especially when angry attack other words are being exchanged—is best summed up as:

"GO TO YOUR ROOM!"

The anger and hard feelings created during lengthy and spiraling exchanges of negative affect are of absolutely no use to anyone. They make us feel more and more distant from one another and create an atmosphere of negativity that can lead to serious distrust in the level of safety we feel in the relationship. This is especially so because the hurt, defensiveness, and competitiveness engendered in angry attack other situations causes people to say extremely harsh, nasty things to one another. So forget any garbage you have ever heard about "getting your anger out" when you find yourself in angry exchanges with your partner. What you must do is shut up and go to another room, leave the house, or do whatever it takes to remove the two of you from the contagious and self-per-

---

4. An excellent reference relating to the need to feel safe is Catherall, Don R. *Emotional Safety: Viewing Couples Through the Lens of Affect*. New York: Routledge, 2007.

petuating nature of anger. While we do need to be aware of our anger, it is more often than not a defense against more vulnerable feelings, as described in Chapter 7.

I well remember a case from early in my practice when a young man called me in tears from a telephone booth several blocks from his apartment. He was distraught because he had walked out on his bride of one year. When I asked about the details, he told me they had been fighting for thirty-six hours in their tiny, one-bedroom apartment. Having grown up around parents whose marriage was completely dysfunctional, his image of a good marriage was one where the two never left one another, especially when angry. He believed he had failed his wife and that his marriage was a disaster. I suggested he go home immediately, since he was clearly no longer angry, and call me soon after arriving home. When he called back, he reported that as soon as he came in the door, they hugged one another and began laughing about the stupid thing that had started the fight. I had no difficulty extracting from him the promise to leave earlier the next time an argument became overheated.

Arguments in cars or other small spaces create the same problem. There is too much resonance of the negative feelings, creating spirals of negativity. One of my patients had to stop driving on the way to "meet the parents" and ask her boyfriend to get out of the car, even though they were miles from anywhere. He would simply not stop talking about a situation from the night before that had caused them both shame, but which they had already discussed for hours. She asked him several times to stop the fruitless discussion, sharing with him her distress, but he could not help himself. She followed Kelly's Rule Number One and took care of herself by making him leave the car. Unfortunately, she eventually had to terminate the relationship because this episode was just one of many in which, too lost in his own feelings, he could not listen to hers. It was therefore almost impossible for them to maintain emotional connection except for very brief moments. The good news is that the wedding invitations had not been mailed.

✦ MORAL: Continuing exchanges of negative feelings only creates more of the same. If you need to get angry, do so, but stop it as soon as you can before it escalates into something extraordinarily damaging.

While removing yourself from the immediate vicinity of your partner begins the process of allowing your brain to cool down, another step is necessary before reuniting. Look for your vulnerable feelings that set off the anger in the first place. It is likely that those feelings were less about some issue and more about how the relationship felt at the moment. For instance, you might ask yourself if you were feeling a lack of interest from your partner, or whether your partner was doing something that blocked your interest in her/him. It is important to discover the impediment that is the real cause of the shame that provoked your anger. Only then can you re-approach one another with vulnerability showing instead of more defensiveness showing. Once you achieve a more vulnerable feeling state, then you can express your negative feelings with sentences like:

"I am feeling we are too distant from one another."

"I would love it if we could spend some more time together."

as opposed to sentences that are attack other and blaming, like:

"I feel that you are a distant person and never have any interest in me."

"I feel that you like to do [*blank*] more than spend time with me."

In other words:

DON'T SAY WHAT HE/SHE DID WRONG; TELL HIM/HER HOW YOU FELT!

Another problem with intense arguments is that each person often rigidly adheres to the notion that they are "right" and the other is "wrong." If you cannot bring yourself to let go of the misconception of who-is-right and who-is-wrong, then your relationship is in big trouble. It is always important to keep in mind that the foundation and motivation behind committed, intimate relationships depends on how we feel about one another. People for whom letting go of the need to be right is impossible present an almost insurmountable problem for their partners. This form of defensiveness, indicative of deep-seated problems with shame, guards their inmost self so closely that emotionally connecting with them is very difficult.

Many years ago, I came across a wonderful sentence, which I have found useful in my work with couples, in, of all places, a science fiction book written by Robert Heinlein—often referred to as the "dean of science fiction writers" in America. He created a character named Lazarus Long, who appeared in five of his books. Lazarus was the eldest member of a family of very long-lived people. His progeny estimated he had lived over 2,000 years. Lazarus was married many times and in long-term relationships with many women, and therefore, he was considered by his family to be an expert on the topic of marriage. Scattered throughout the 1973 book, *Time Enough for Love*, are the sayings of Lazarus Long. This one about marriage caught my eye:

IN A FAMILY ARGUMENT, IF IT TURNS OUT YOU ARE RIGHT, APOLOGIZE AT ONCE!

When I encounter couples caught in the who-is-right/who-is-wrong dilemma in therapy, I suggest they pay attention to this saying. It often helps them understand that continuation of this defensive posture can only produce impediment to emotional connection. After all, if someone must be right, then someone must be wrong, making shame in at least one person inevitable. Furthermore, if being "right" is more important to you than positive feelings in your relationship, then you need to consider the possibility that you have a significant amount of shame in your personality. Warm, loving, emotionally connected and intimate relationships are not possible until one deals with such shame. This is a situation where it is *wrong to be right!*

One unanticipated benefit of sharing the words of Lazarus Long with couples is how many of them eventually use it to inject humor into difficult situations. Quite a few have told me that they often begin apologizing during a heated argument, which gets them laughing and short-circuits the argument. This is a wonderful way to mutualize and minimize negative feelings. It indicates a mutual awareness that in the practice of the art of intimacy, the "need to be right" is contraindicated.

Mission 6c: Mutualize and Minimize the Inhibition of Feelings

As implied in Mission 6b, the sharing of feelings is no easy task when they are negative. As indicated at other places in this book, there are also internalized cultural and familial directives that prohibit openness about our feelings. For instance, I know of more than one man who refuses to share feelings of fear with his wife lest she think him a "wimp" and a coward. There are also many people who have been shamed out of expressing anger with their significant other. Once taught it is not "nice" to be angry or to confront someone directly with negative feelings, people hide or suppress such feelings. And, as described in Chapter 7, expressions like "big boys don't cry" have so infested the male psyche in Western culture that most men have learned to get angry at any sign of vulnerability or weakness rather than cry or show the weakness. As strange as it may seem, anger inhibits the expression of feelings. It both disguises the real feelings of the person who is angry and scares their partner into silence.

I teach couples to think of anger as a symptom. It is like a high fever when you have the flu. The fever is the body's response to all of the nasty things influenza viruses do inside of us. One must treat the fever symptomatically because it can be dangerous if it produces febrile seizures. However, the real problem is the virus. Once you get rid of the virus with antiviral agents, the fever goes away. Anger can be just as dangerous since it may lead to violence against the self and/or the other. Sometimes it requires treatment with anti-anger medications. Nevertheless, until one gets relief from the more vulnerable feelings motivating the anger, it will not go away. The bottom line of how to think about anger is:

WHEN YOU ARE ANGRY, YOU ARE A VULNERABLE MESS INSIDE.

Missions 1 through 6b contain methods of becoming more aware of our real feelings or the defenses against them. Once a couple begins to carry out these missions as joint activities, as if the two are allies, not enemies, gradually—because it takes many repetitions to get it right—they will feel safer about exposing their more vulnerable sides. It is important to note the growth potential in what I refer to as the "debriefing" period after a disagreement. By this I mean the time period, once things have cooled down, when couples reconnect. This is when some couples engage in "make-up sex." It is the best time for people to share the vulnerable feelings that led to the defenses that led to the fight. Opening up one's inmost self—when it feels safe to do so—leads to a stronger emotional connection because of the new insights provided by such exposure. The debriefing period is critical for the full development of the art of intimacy because it is here that one learns the most about the rewards of self-exposure.

When couples begin to utilize the information described in this book, they report that while they have not stopped having fights, the fights last for shorter periods and the debriefing sessions are more and more rewarding. This is a good sign that things are getting better because the couple is less fearful of disagreements. It means they are in the process of developing new patterns to help them deal with negative emotion rather than avoiding its expression.

I have never been under the illusion that the end of fighting or disagreements is essential to a successful marriage or, for that matter, to successful therapy for a troubled marriage. I believe that the ability to be angry at one another without fear of the relationship falling apart is a healthy sign. I make the analogy that it is impossible to live in close proximity to another person without stepping on each other's toes from time to time. One needs to be able to say "ouch" clearly in order to get relief (and follow Kelly's Rule Number One). Either an inability to say ouch or the striking out with angry reprisals represents a failure in minimizing the expression of true feelings. As such, this becomes an impediment to emotional connection. After all, if you love someone, you do not want to step on their toes. Furthermore, you want them to let you know if you do so you can stop hurting them. It is normal for people to say ouch in a loud voice if it really hurts.

Anyone who does not share their feelings, perhaps because they are stuck in the shame defense of withdrawal, impedes the interest of their partner in getting closer to them. I have seen quite a few relationships die a slow death from the distance that inevitably follows chronic withholding of feelings. Eventually the partner of an emotionally silent person must withdraw their interest to protect themselves from the constant experience of shame. Ironically, the same thing happens inside of the silent one because they too experience shame and impediment to emotional connection from their lack of openness.

✦ MORAL: The Surgeon General has determined that failure to minimize the inhibition of affect is hazardous to your relational health.

Mission 7: Forget the Idea that Everything Must Be Resolved

The tenets of the Central Blueprint rule all relationships. If a couple utilizes them consciously and proactively, then the resolution of "issues" becomes less important than how the two people feel about one another. Can this be possible? Can people live together with unresolved issues? I believe so. Here are some further thoughts along these same lines:

Political Opposites: can a couple be happy if he is a Republican and she is a Democrat? Or does happiness depend on all of us becoming either Republocrats or Demopublicans?

Religion: what if one is Jewish and the other Catholic? Or one is religiously devout and the other agnostic?

These are potentially powerful differences. Religious differences have caused many wars and much suffering and death—perhaps even more deaths than any other known cause. And, especially during election years in the USA, the antipathy and venom displayed by political candidates toward their opponent's person, ideals, and standards is often disgusting.

In spite of this, we all know of couples with successful relationships who belong to different political parties or have disparate religious ideologies. Some have lived together for many years without ever resolving these "differences." This is no mean feat. Political or religious ideology is a significant part of anyone's personality. In addition, such ideologies usually remain unchanged throughout one's adult life. However, individuals can overcome political, religious, and cultural differences if the couple's emotional connection is properly nurtured and maintained. True intimacy triumphs over differing intellectual matters.

If these powerful issues can be overcome, then the many little minor annoyances, things the other does that we do not like, can also be overcome. Have you ever noticed that some days these little things the other does seem more bothersome than issues one might consider "more important"? If you watch carefully how connected you feel to your partner, you will notice that during times of relative disconnection, all the little things seem very annoying. This is actually very useful information about how much shame you are experiencing at the time—in other words, how much impediment to emotional connection is present. Moreover, it is interesting to note how often I have heard that after a positive sexual encounter, those little things do not seem annoying at all. Once people reconnect emotionally, issues become less important.

Over the past four decades, I have seen a number of couples go through seemingly insurmountable crises. The "issues" creating such crises have ranged from extramarital affairs to drug and alcohol addictions to other forms of betrayal. During the crisis, the future of the relationship often appeared to hang in the balance. But when these were people who loved one another, they saw the importance of working hard in therapy. Many used the crisis to learn new ways of connecting emotionally—ways that were more effective and provided them with greater resilience when new crises arose. This generated new emotional tools that made the relationship feel safe to them. The individuals involved grew emotionally through these difficult times, shedding defenses against shame that were often the cause of the crisis. The "issues" were never resolved because no one can go back in time and have a "do-over." However, the greater facility with the art of intimacy that developed during such crises created a consistency of positive feelings in the present such that the issue and its negative feelings moved into the background—for sure, never to be forgotten, but no longer creating impediment to emotional connection.

When Home Remedies Fail

There can come a time when you cannot "do it yourselves," and self-help books are unable to provide satisfactory insights into how to make things better between you and your partner. More often than not, while there is shame about seeking therapy, it is usually better than the alternative. Because we all carry blind spots about our shame and our defensive behaviors, using the eyes of a therapist to guide us is more likely to make us better equipped to deal with problems in our patterns of relating.

Finding a couples therapist with whom you and your significant other are comfortable is not always an easy task. However, it is the most critical part of couples therapy. Because the process of therapy always involves exposing things about which people feel shame, both of you must feel that the therapist is unbiased and provides a safe environment in which to expose vulnerable feelings. The good news is that there are literally hundreds of different theoretical systems of couples therapy, guaranteeing that you should be able to find a therapist and a style that suits the two of you. Some therapy systems are more popular than others depending on how well their proponents have marketed the theory through the publishing of books and the use of radio and TV. You can even find couples therapists by searching the Internet, which provides a dazzling array of choices and some interesting ideas about how to make a selection.

I think the best way to find a therapist—couples or individual—is to talk to friends and family to see if any of them have been in therapy and if they would recommend their therapist. Your shame about seeking therapy can, of course, get in the way of doing this. However, it is worth considering because hiding from friends and/or family that your relationship is in distress may seem like it helps but it never does. (The Beatles were right: we get by with a little help from our friends.) If any friends or family have been to a therapist about whom they are very positive, consulting that therapist is a good way to begin your search for someone who feels "right" to both of you. But do not stop there if you are not comfortable. Have no shame about "shopping" for a therapist. It is a decision that can have serious implications for the rest of your life—either positive *or* negative.

From the perspective of affect script psychology as presented in this book, here are several ideas about couples therapy that might help you with your decision:

1) Do not seek a therapist to act as a "referee." You will never con-

nect better emotionally if you're engaged in some sort of contest where one of you has to be right and the other wrong. And if an unenlightened therapist chooses sides, big trouble will ensue. If, on the other hand, the therapist declares you both to be right, that therapist is on the right track. You **are** both right about what you feel, even if you are unclear about the origins of those feelings. Feelings are facts; what you make of those facts is open to question.

The predominant feeling present when two people finally seek couples therapy is usually anger. As you now know, this is a defense against shame, a mechanism to protect people from feeling too vulnerable. Therapists not tricked by anger recognize the vulnerable feelings behind it. Expert therapists create an environment in which you both feel safe. They draw out your vulnerable feelings and establish an emotional setting in which you can expose your inmost selves to one another. You will leave that person's office feeling better connected emotionally.

2) If the therapist passively sits by while you and your partner fight and become angrier with one another, assume that the therapist has the outdated notion that getting your anger out is necessary and useful. Such a therapist is unwittingly in collusion with attack other defenses against shame. All that will be accomplished in such a setting is an increase in shame defenses, further emotional disconnection leading to more shame, and the feeling that you are not in a safe environment. You will leave that person's office still feeling emotionally disconnected.

3) All couples therapists have some system of helping people improve their communication skills. I worry about therapeutic systems that insist on people learning how to "fight fair." In my experience, it is extremely difficult for people who are angrily defending against shame to engage in a fair fight. I actively intervene in any angry exchanges that take place in my office, often by commenting, "I'm sure you get all the practice you need while fighting at home."

My ultimate goal is not that the couple will never fight again (to suggest such a thing is therapist error guaranteed to create shame), but that improvement in their awareness and sharing of vulnerable feelings will create a much safer atmosphere. The safer they feel, the more they grow as individuals and as a couple, and the more they feel like allies, not enemies. The more they grow, the easier it is to give up the need to be right or the need to be angry for long periods of time. You know you are with a competent therapist when your fights last for shorter and shorter periods of time before you make up, and when those fights decrease in frequency. Tongue in cheek, I tell couples that the ideal fight lasts less than five minutes, and that it takes less than another five minutes to reconnect emotionally.

4) Do not stay in couples therapy with a therapist who allows you and/or your spouse to spend time complaining about the other. Even complaining in a calm, logical voice is attack other. The complainer is stuck in defenses against shame and may not even be aware that their complaints create further impediment to emotional connection. A highly respected teacher of mine, Edward Taylor, M.D., taught me a technique I sometimes use to deal with complaining. If I'm struggling with a couple, or with one member of a couple who cannot stop complaining, I step in and tell them they should get all the complaints they have about the other out on the table in the next twenty minutes; after that, complaining will not be permitted because it is useless, and, as a result, I will actively stop it for the rest of time they are in therapy with me.

5) The negative emotions motivating a couple to seek therapy are useful because they signal the need for change, but they are painful and difficult to manage. If, during couples therapy sessions, the therapist cannot help create moments of positive emotion between you and your partner, something is very wrong either with your relationship or with the therapist. Persistent negative emotion during therapy sessions makes things worse. It does not generate the sense of being in a safe place. No one wants to open up and be more vulnerable in an unsafe environment. If you do not feel positive emotions at times during your treatment sessions, I suggest you seek out another therapist. In this same light, a therapist with a sense of humor is a great asset.

6) The new information about shame presented in this book is critical to an understanding of what makes relationships work and how best to manage one's emotional connection. Many couples therapists know about and work with shame intuitively, even if they do not clearly understand its triggering mechanism. I feel strongly that knowing the details of the innate affect shame is vitally important for a clear understanding of how relationships work and how they fail. I always teach couples these details. The feedback I get from them confirms my impression that they find it useful. If you find the material in this book helpful and wish to learn more about affect script psychology, please go online to the Tomkins Institute website at www.tomkins.org.

CHAPTER 11

SEX & SHAME

In Chapter 4, I explored the general features of potential impediments to emotional connection. Two kinds of impediments surface so regularly in the treatment of troubled couples that I would be remiss not to touch on them in slightly more detail. I do so here and in the next chapter with the realization that I cannot do justice to either topic. Each undoubtedly deserves an entire book.

To place the topic of sex and shame in proper perspective, I quote two paragraphs from *Shame and Pride: Affect, Sex, and the Birth of the Self*, Donald Nathanson's pioneering work on shame in human sexuality:

> We are excited by sexual arousal and calmed when released by orgasm from that arousal. Every aspect of sexuality is capable of triggering intense experiences of the positive affects interest-excitement and enjoyment-joy. Sexual arousal is accompanied by fantasy, by images of scenes in which our sexual wishes will be gratified. To the extent that we can get others to become players in the scenes, we will share with them both our excitement and our release. Sexual success, for man or woman, brings pride.
>
> Yet the human is so constructed that whenever that other person falters for so much as a moment in his or her willingness to resonate with our arousal and its accompanying positive affect, we will experience shame. No matter how sensitive our sexual partner may be, no matter how precisely attuned to the nuances of our arousal, it is impossible for any two aroused and excited individuals to match perfectly each other's patterns of arousal. Always, inevitably, invariably, our experience of sexual arousal

must meet with some sort or degree of impediment. Shame affect, the painfully amplified analogue of this impediment, is as much an accompaniment of sexuality as the positive affect by which we prefer to know it better.[5]

Nathanson, in the language of affect psychology, reaffirms a truth we have all known for most of our lives: we are very vulnerable when it comes to our sexuality. We can alternate rapidly between the highs of feeling a wonderful sense of pride and joy in our sexiness to the lows of feeling a devastating sense of humiliation that we are sexually defective or undesirable. This has extremely important consequences for intimate relationships and the ebb and flow of the emotional connection with our significant other.

There are two facts about sex and shame that are worth keeping in mind:

All problems with sexuality involve shame!

They trigger many of the shame family of emotions as well as Compass of Shame defenses; and therefore,

Sexual problems are always impediments to emotional connection.

It is important to note that, in a circular fashion, impediments to emotional connection triggering shame also act as impediments to sexual interest and enjoyment. In other words, shame about sex causes problems with emotional connection and shame from difficulty in connecting emotionally causes problems with sex.

While there is obviously more than one kind of sexual problem that brings couples into treatment, the most common cause of long-term impediment is the inability of the two people involved to talk openly and constructively about what is troubling them sexually. Many people in Western culture, in spite of the so-called "sexual revolution," still have significant shame about their sexuality. This impedes their ability to talk about it, especially when it comes to exposing their own sexual desires, fantasies, and needs. Sexual difficulties, therefore, often become the "elephant in the room." This contributes to a serious failure in the ability of the couple to mutualize and minimize the inhibition of negative feelings. It creates an ever-expanding communication problem that I—a science fiction and astrophysics fan—have likened to a black hole in space.

5. Page 286

My amateur conceptualization of a black hole is that its center contains so much mass and, as a result, a gravitational field so powerful that not even light can escape from it. Furthermore, its gravity engulfs any object that gets too close to it and pulls it out of the light. This is exactly what I see happen with couples who cannot discuss their sexuality. Their shame about sex creates a powerful force inhibiting not only discussion of the sexual problem itself but also the many things that surround sexual functioning, physical contact with one another, and (perhaps carrying the metaphor too far) the ability to shine light on—expose—important aspects of oneself to one's partner.

If this becomes a regular pattern, couples need to seek therapy, either with a general couples therapist or with a sex therapist, in order to have a safe place that minimizes the risk involved in exposing sexual feelings. They must find a way to discuss sexual feelings openly because unresolved sexual problems are a major impediment to emotional connection. They create chronic shame and emotional distance. However, because of shame about sex and shame about discussing sex, too many couples avoid getting help. While I have not seen any convincing studies, I suspect that sexual problems, many of which remain hidden from researchers because of shame, are a prominent cause of the shame that leads to divorce.

I have already mentioned the most common cause of sexual problems, but it is worth looking into it a bit further because it *must* occur in every relationship. Simply stated, it is: *sexual frequency in all successful, committed, long-term relationships diminishes over time.* The primary motivator of interest-excitement in one's partner, in their body and the sexual pleasures we experience together, is novelty. By definition, a successful relationship, one that lasts, becomes less novel. Therefore, after varying periods of time unique to each relationship, the level of interest and hence the motivation to engage in sexual activity lessens. This is true whether there are other sexual problems or not. An elderly gentleman once said to me, "If you put a penny in a jar each time you have sex during the first year of marriage and take one out each time you have sex after that year, you will never empty the jar."

Whether or not this method of saving pennies is true for your relationship, it is a simple fact of nature bestowed upon us by our biology that sexual frequency in a relationship diminishes with the passage of time. While everyone knows this to be true and most are even able to accept it as a simple fact of life, it still is likely to cause shame. Why? *Because it is almost inevitable that the sexual drive of one of the partners remains higher than that of the other.* It would be a lot easier if both people lost interest in sex at exactly the same time. But, while this does occur, it is seldom the case.

In relationships where both people are very skilled, open, and have little or no shame communicating about their sexual feelings, this problem of different levels of interest in sex is minimized. For instance, some work out an arrangement whereby, when one feels interested in sex, she or he tells the other, and, if the less interested partner is agreeable, they engage in sexual activity. An interesting benefit of such an arrangement is that the person with low or absent sex drive often reports that as things progress, they too become aroused, even to the point of being able to have an orgasm. Such couples exhibit a powerful ability to remain emotionally connected in the face of what could be a serious problem with shame about sex. They know how to mutualize and maximize positive feelings, mutualize and minimize negative feelings, and mutualize and minimize the inhibition of feelings.

Couples less skilled at remaining emotionally connected have significant shame invade their relationship in similar situations. When the other turns away sexual advances or suggestions, the sexually interested partner *will* have shame triggered. This response can range anywhere from mild shame to deep humiliation. Depending upon the preexisting shame vulnerability of that person—a trait that is often referred to as their level of self-esteem—they can feel anything from mildly rejected, hurt, frustrated, and disappointed to sexually defective and deeply humiliated by their apparent lack of sexual appeal to their partner.

To complicate matters further, the partner who has little or no sexual interest frequently has shame problems of their own. Their shame is not triggered by an impediment to sexual interest, but rather by an impediment to an image of themselves. Their shame comes from the belief that to be a "normal" healthy adult they *should* be interested in sex. The intensity of their shame depends upon their preexisting shame vulnerability or self-esteem and the degree to which their partner shames them for their lack of interest.

While it is completely normal for both people to experience shame when the passage of time reduces sexual interest, it should be clear from the ideas advanced throughout this book that, if not dealt with properly, this simple fact of nature can ruin a relationship. The shame triggered in both people can lead to Compass of Shame spirals and chronic emotional disconnection. And, of course, such disconnection triggers shame of its own that further impedes sexual interest and magnifies the problem.

The same set of problems can arise if the lack of sexual interest of one partner is temporary, caused by ordinary life circumstances. For instance, a woman may have her sexual drive momentarily obliterated by hormonal changes associated with pregnancy and childbirth. Or both partners may be utterly exhausted from the lack of sleep caring for a new-born, especially if they have other children. (Tomkins stressed that positive affect is dependent upon one's energy level; low energy states make the triggering of interest-excitement very difficult and hence reduce the desire to engage in sex even when some sexual drive is present.) Or the hormonal changes associated with menopause can make a woman disinterested in sex. Physical illness, job stressors, mourning the loss of a loved one, or a myriad of other situations, can create a temporary loss of interest in sex. Even if a couple has had a satisfying sex life before any of these things happen, and even if the one whose sex drive is still intact is completely understanding and empathetic about what is happening to the other, shame will inevitably be triggered.

There is, of course, shame about many other sexual problems besides diminished or absent interest in sex. The shame of erectile dysfunction, for example, has created a huge market for medications that counteract it. (In both personal and professional settings, men have shared with me their willingness to risk the side effects of taking erectile dysfunction medications every day to avoid embarrassment "just in case" a sexual encounter takes place.) Premature ejaculation, the inability to achieve orgasm, the belief that one's sexual fantasies are weird, the desire to look at pornography, the absence of the desire to look at pornography, and issues related to masturbation are just a few of the other sexually related issues that can create shame for a couple.

It has been my goal in this book to make clear that shame is a normal, natural response when there is any impediment to the positive feelings of interest or enjoyment, and that awareness of shame and the shame family of emotions is critical for relational health. Nowhere is this truer than in the arena of a couple's sexual life. But, as I stated in the introduction to this book, being aware of shame as it relates to one's sexuality or any other aspect of one's relationship does not mean that shame will disappear. Shame related to sexual interest appears at the beginning, middle, and end of all relationships and only vanishes if the sexual temperature of both partners reaches absolute zero. The ability to be aware of why, when and how shame is present, coupled with the ability to share those feelings and insights with one's partner, opening up about one's most vulnerable self, is the only way to keep potential problems presented by sexually triggered shame from ruining a relationship.

CHAPTER 12

MEDICATION FOR INTIMACY?

In Chapter 5, I touched very briefly on the topic of mental illness as a potential impediment to emotional connection. The proper treatment of any so-called mental illness is necessary when it begins to interfere with a relationship. In the next few pages, I want to share with you some aspects of my experience treating couples when one or both of the partners suffered from what medical science currently labels as a "mental illness."

When I first began doing psychotherapy in the late 1960s, I believed that talk therapy could "cure" most people with psychological problems. If the person was interested in the causes of their problems, by helping them analyze and come to terms with issues from their past and assisting them to change things in their present relationship, I believed that interaction with a caring psychotherapist was all that was needed. This was in the days when the nature-versus-nurture debate about the origins of mental illness leaned heavily toward nurture—and, as a result, we accused mothers of all kinds of terrible things. One researcher even proposed that certain highly intellectual mothers with professional careers were "cold" around their infants and that this caused autism in a number of these children. In that same era, some researchers also believed that schizophrenia was caused by mothers who placed their children in something called "double bind" situations, which today we would probably dub "lose-lose" situations. Some members of the mental health professions gave these women the label "schizophrenogenic" mothers.

Today, although we have only begun to understand some of the complicated biological processes that impact the brains of people with autism or schizophrenia, we are quite certain that biology (nature) is the true cause of autism and schizophrenia. The understanding that biological problems can damage relationships has gone through a similar transformation. We now recognize that "love is not enough." That is to say, if one's partner is severely depressed, highly anxious, has problems with addiction, or suffers from another of the biologically based mental disorders, loving them will not cure them. Many, if not all, of these disorders can ruin a relationship. If we do not properly understand them and treat them medically, they become major impediments to emotional connection and create persistent shame in both partners.

To best understand the material that follows, I once again—and I promise this is the last time—strongly suggest reading "A Primer of Affect Psychology" in Appendix I. In the Primer, I use the term *affect system* to distinguish it and its function from several other functional brain systems. The function of the affect system is to provide information about the most important stimuli going on both outside and inside us so that our attention focuses on the things that matter the most. Simply stated, the affect system works by identifying any important stimulus picked up by our sensory system and *amplifying* it so that it triggers one of the nine innate affects. We become consciously aware of that stimulus when—and only when—a stimulus triggers an affect.

As is the case with every other organ system in our bodies, things can go wrong with the biology of the brain. Sometimes we are born with the defect; sometimes it develops as we age. Studies of the so-called depressive and anxiety disorders, as well as bipolar disorder, for instance, point to problems with several of the brain's chemical agents known as neurotransmitters. To date, research has identified over sixty neurotransmitters, including serotonin, dopamine, glutamate, acetylcholine, norepinephrine, and GABA. The current belief is that faulty regulation of the levels of these chemicals or the brain's responses to them contributes to or causes a number of problems with feelings, emotions, and moods. The way in which chemical or other kinds of alterations in the brain change a person emotionally is by causing irregularities in the normal functioning of the affect system.

I will focus here on how two regularly occurring affect system irregularities impact emotional connection and the practice of the art of intimacy. In the first, the affect system generates excess negative feelings when there is no external cause or trigger for such feelings—nothing in the person's environment is the problem. Instead, some process in the brain that has gone haywire and will not shut off continually triggers bad feelings. In the second, the amplifying mechanism of the affect system is faulty and causes much more intense emotional responses to events than would be expected. In many situations, both of these problems occur simultaneously.

One could liken the first set of problems to constant brain "noise," somewhat analogous to ringing in the ears that is overly loud and never stops. Such conditions act as a steady-state stimulus of a dense nature and therefore continually trigger the innate affect *distress-anguish*. Because it never stops, what the person experiences is chronic distress with gradual intensification toward anguish. This is the primary source of the emotional syndrome called depression. When distress-anguish of sufficient intensity and duration persists, it dominates all aspects of a person's thinking and feeling life. The depressed person then sees everything as if they were wearing a pair of glasses coated with distress. As a result, they perceive even the simplest of tasks as distressing to the point of being overwhelming. For instance, it can feel as if one must muster the mental energy to climb Mt. Everest when the only chore at hand is to take out the trash.

Those who have experienced such an affect system glitch will never tell a depressed person to "pull yourself up by the bootstraps and get on with it, you'll feel fine." They know this is not possible because, having been through it, it is likely that they have tried the "bootstrap" method and found it useless. Furthermore, having experienced intense shame at being unable to accomplish what they once did easily without even thinking about it, they know with certainty that such admonitions from others only create more shame and with it more distress in an unending cycle of terribly dark feelings.

In direct contrast to those whose distress-anguish is from obvious, unremittingly negative situations in their daily lives, such as chronic hunger, chronic work stress, an abusive relationship, chronic illness, chronic pain, or having to live in a dysfunctional family, people who have biologically caused distress-anguish cannot "see" the glitch in their brain. Regardless of the fact that such biologically induced illnesses have no visible component, when one experiences these negative feelings, the cognitive (thinking) part of the brain is compelled to seek out and identify reasons why we feel bad. In situations where we correctly ascertain the cause of our bad feelings, we can sometimes make changes that help us feel better. This is *not* possible, however, if what is making us feel bad is invisible. In this case, we are likely to blame our bad feelings on things that have nothing to do with why we really feel that way.

A comparable situation can occur with any illness whose biological nature is invisible. For instance, in my early fifties, I developed a slight tremor in my hands. As it got worse, I felt more and more distress because my cognitive system mistakenly invented the idea that I was in the early stages of the same inherited familial tremor from which mother suffered. To make matters even worse, I believed that there was little I could do about it except try anti-tremor medications, all of which had failed to help my mother and all of which had caused her to feel overly sedated. As the tremor worsened, it became impossible to hold my putter still at critical moments in golf matches (blocking my interest in doing well, hence triggering shame). When a few other symptoms began to appear, it finally became clear to me that I needed to consult my physician. Simple blood tests indicated I was suffering from hyperthyroidism. I had an excess of thyroid hormone causing everything in my body to be overactive. I felt immense relief that I had a treatable condition. Once treated, my hands stopped shaking and my putter began to behave. Needless to say, I could not "see" the excess thyroid hormone in my body, but this did not stop my cognitive system from developing an explanation that I believed. This "wrong" reason caused me to avoid getting medical attention as early as I should have.

(Unfortunately, as of this writing, medical science has yet to develop simple blood tests that accurately identify the source of many of the biologically caused problems of the affect system. However, anyone who begins to experience significant distress-anguish and feels depressed or unable to muster any interest or enjoyment in life should consult their primary care physician. Many treatable illnesses cause problems with the affect system and generate distress, fear, or other negative feelings, as well as loss of interest in life. The vast majority originate in parts of the body other than the brain and are identifiable by currently available diagnostic tests.)

How does depression from distress-anguish that never shuts off create impediment to emotional connection? I implied one way in the story about my hyperthyroidism. A depressed person seeking an answer to why they feel depressed often places the blame on their partner. This is not at all surprising. After all, there is no perfect relationship. Inevitably, even in the best of relationships, little things one's partner does are annoying from time to time. When depressed, it is very difficult to ignore things about one's partner that one usually overlooks without much difficulty. Furthermore, when one sees the world through glasses coated with distress, we perceive almost everything that happens as distressing. The depressed partner compounds the problem by misinterpreting even little events and attributing to them an **intentionality** that does not exist. For instance, the nondepressed partner may innocently rattle the newspaper at the breakfast table, an action the depressed partner finds so distressing that they criticize the other for doing it on purpose. The intensity of the negative feelings generated by such interactions is a clear and extremely powerful impediment to emotional connection.

To complicate matters further, constant distress-anguish inhibits the ability of the affect system to generate interest-excitement and enjoyment-joy. The person who feels bad has a hard time feeling good. This creates a diminished level of interest in their partner and in their ability to be interested in their partner's interest in them. They withdraw into the self and impede emotional connection. They cannot connect with their partner and their partner cannot connect with them. The shame from this blockage adds to the negative feelings of the depressed person and further increases their distress. Consequently, what may have begun as a misinterpretation that their partner is the source of their negative feelings can become true if the partner withdraws or attacks other to defend against their own feelings of shame—a self-validating response.

An increase in an individual's shame affect accompanies almost all depressive syndromes. It is open to debate whether the same biologic glitch that triggers the excessive distress-anguish also triggers excessive shame affect or whether the shame results from impediments to one's interest in functioning normally or whether the problem results from a combination of the two. The words and behaviors of people suffering from this excess shame cause observers to say that they have "low self-esteem" or are suffering from feelings of guilt—the shame/fear emotion. This is evidence that the shame-prone person is engaged in the Compass of Shame defense of *attack self*. No matter the cause, excess shame or vulnerability to shame makes people very rejection sensitive. This is an example of the second affect system glitch mentioned earlier: over-amplification of events with greater emotional response than would be expected.

As discussed in Appendix I, one of the functions of the affect system involves the process of amplification of affects. The emotional responses of people in whom this function has gone awry are either too great or too little. It is as if the volume control on your radio has a mind of its own. No matter how carefully you attempt to change the volume, it plays the music either too loud or too soft. For instance, some people with depression feel little or nothing when things happen. They commonly say things like "I feel dead inside." Others who respond with overly intense emotional responses often say things like "I can't control myself. I cry for hours or become enraged or feel completely rejected by every little thing that happens." Attempts at emotional connection by or with someone experiencing an out-of-control affect system is sometimes difficult and at other times impossible. This is true no matter the cause of the affect system glitch. Any illness with effects on the brain impacts the affect system. This includes things such as diabetes, multiple sclerosis, hyper- or hypothyroidism, depression, bipolar disorder, and schizophrenia, to name just a few.

Here is an example of what can happen: A man in his late forties recently consulted me. His employer, a former patient of mine, referred him. This typically hard-working, reliable gentleman was deeply disturbed and terribly ashamed when his employer caught him in a series of lies about his job performance. The patient reported to me that he had gradually been losing interest in going to work. He experienced intense distress and fear each morning at the thought of leaving the house. His job involved daily visits to business locations which housed machinery leased by his employer. He would analyze the efficiency of each machine and recalibrate it if necessary. At first, he began skipping his morning visits. However, as he felt worse, he began staying at home for days at a time while still reporting to his office by phone that he was making his normal rounds. His employer eventually discovered the truth and confronted him. Because he had been a reliable employee for many years, his employer sensed that something more than simple deceit was the problem and referred him to me.

The patient was certain his problems were "mental." In his opinion, a problem with his wife was at the core of his troubles. His theory was that he began to feel bad when his wife's job suddenly required her to spend four days a week in another city. He would take her to the train on Sunday evenings and return home feeling lonely. He expressed to me that he had always been overly dependent on her. He trusted her completely and did not believe she was being unfaithful to him. In his opinion, his lonely feelings gradually led him to begin crying at the drop of a hat over silly things. This crying and sadness, he believed, made him feel tired, run-down, and uncomfortable about leaving home in the morning. He began to spend hours on the phone crying to his wife about his loneliness. She found herself in a terrible bind because she loved her job and did not want to give it up in order to take care of him. All of these factors created an impediment to their normally positive emotional connection. Her shame led her to attack him as weak and pitiful. His shame led him to attack himself as weak and pitiful.

When he consulted me for an evaluation, he was very embarrassed about his condition and the fact that he had lied to his employer. He seemed a very good man who was unable to control his emotions despite years of normal functioning in almost all aspects of his life. I listened carefully to his explanation of his marital problems, but I sensed something more might be at play. When he related his medical history and the fact that he was on thyroid medication for hypothyroidism (a thyroid that is not making enough hormone), I sent him for blood tests. Depression is one of the symptoms of hypothyroidism, as is fatigue, feeling run-down and out of energy. His test results shocked me. He had the lowest amount of thyroid hormone of any patient I had ever treated. I was amazed that he could function at all. I referred him to an endocrinologist who immediately increased his thyroid hormone. After several months, he began to feel better. While he remained unhappy about his wife's work situation, it did not bother him as much. He stopped obsessing about it and no longer cried so easily. His distress and fatigue in the mornings abated and he was able to go to work every day without difficulty. He declared himself no longer "depressed." In his last report to me, he said that he and his wife were back in love and feeling wonderful about each other.

This man's case represents a situation where medicine was clearly necessary. The medical literature well documents that hypothyroidism causes "depression." For the most part, however, that same literature remains uniformed about affect psychology. Were it so informed, it would describe how the effects of low amounts of thyroid hormone on the cells of the body and brain trigger continual distress-anguish—the root cause of the syndrome of depression. This man's hypothyroid-induced depressive symptoms of crying, feeling intensely lonely, and feeling so uncomfortable in the morning, also triggered significant amounts of shame. He hid his problems from his employer by not telling him about the problem—because he had so much shame about his condition—and compounded his shame by lying. A similar shame cycle appeared in his relationship with his wife. The only "talking" therapy I administered during the three sessions we had together was in the form of education about his condition and its effects on his affect system. Medical treatment with the correct dose of thyroid hormone took away the trigger for his distress-anguish. All of his symptoms vanished.

This case also demonstrates how physical conditions that cause glitches in the affect system create marital misunderstandings. The negative feelings from an affect system problem led this man to believe his wife's absence was THE cause of all that was wrong with him, and that he was a weak, overly dependent person. This misinterpretation impeded emotional connection with his wife, sending them into a Compass of Shame spiral. All the misattributions of the cause of his problems also vanished with the administration of the correct dose of thyroid hormone. His relationship with his wife returned to its previously positive state without psychotherapeutic intervention. (Had this man sought help through psychotherapy rather than receiving treatment for his hypothyroidism, his emotional condition would have deteriorated further. Not only would the effects of the physical illness have worsened, but he would also have begun to experience significant shame when his emotional state failed to improve with psychotherapy.)

I believe the frequency of such biologically induced affect system problems is much greater than generally recognized. Untreated physical illnesses and conditions, with their capacity to trigger continuing distress-anguish and shame, are frequent sources of impediment to emotional connection. Without treatment—be it with medicine or other forms of medical intervention—prolonged impediment to emotional connection and the resulting shame dynamics seriously compromise relationship longevity. Furthermore, most physicians have neither the time nor the training to talk with couples about the impact illnesses have on relationships. Sometimes the damage to the relationship is such that it lingers even after successful treatment of the medical condition.

This is especially true of the illnesses currently labeled "mental illnesses." Their impact on the affect system is powerful. They result from physical glitches in the brain that induce either chronic or ever-cycling states of distress or fear or shame or combinations of these negative affects. Such glitches are invisible to someone suffering from them, as was the lack of thyroid hormone not visible to the patient just described. The difference is that there is a simple blood test to measure the amount of thyroid hormone in someone's body, whereas the same is not yet true in the case of most mental illnesses. Because research has yet to discover simple ways to identify the causes of mental illnesses, unlike my patient who was greatly relieved when I told him about his thyroid test results, those with mental illnesses suffer from shame and uncertainty about their condition. They, and others close to them, often wonder whether they "really" have something medically wrong or whether, as so many still believe, it is "just in their head" and they should pull themselves up by their bootstraps and get moving, and they will be fine.

Furthermore, despite widespread educational attempts by the mental health profession, there remains a general cultural bias against the use of the psychotropic medications currently available for the treatment of mental illnesses. I would be the first to agree with anyone who argues that these medications are imperfect. They do not always work and they can cause extremely unpleasant side effects. Nor do we fully understand what their long-term side effects might be. However, I have improved the quality of dozens of marriages by reducing chronic distress, fear, and/or shame with the judicious use of these medications. A great deal of research into the genetic and other causes of disorders that directly impact the brain remains undone. I am optimistic that in the future medical science will prevail and perfect both the prevention and treatment of mental illness. When that day comes, there will be diagnostic tests for mental illness as simple as the blood tests for thyroid disease. This will go a long way toward reducing the stigma—and the shame—of mental illness, the belief that it is some kind of moral or personal weakness in its sufferers. Moreover, it will provide us with specific treatments that are as safe as replacing the low levels of thyroid hormone in someone with hypothyroidism.

In the meantime, there are grave relationship implications for illnesses like depression, bipolar disorder, ADHD, premenstrual syndrome (PMS)—or its more severe form, premenstrual dysphoric disorder (PMDD)—to mention just a few. Medicine can help. For example, the chronic distress that often leads to irritability and anger in someone who is depressed is a powerful impediment to emotional connection. The depression triggers impediment in two ways because it lowers the capacity of its sufferer both to experience interest and to show interest. Therefore, the depressed partner cannot feel the interest of the other, while the other feels no interest coming their way from their depressed partner. Shame is triggered in both, causing each to feel rejected. In those situations where neither partner is aware that a biologically induced glitch is the source of the negative feelings, both usually misinterpret the cause of the negative feelings.

The most common—and completely logical—misinterpretation in these situations is that he or she no longer loves me. After all, if one no longer feels the interest of the other directed toward them, one does not feel loved by that person. People with very deep depressions are, in fact, unable to love. To feel love, one must be able to experience the positive affects of interest-excitement and enjoyment-joy. This is not possible when the intensity of distress-anguish induced by biological defects reaches too high a level. In such cases, the person not only cannot love another very well, they cannot love themselves either. Antidepressant medication that stops chronic distress restores a person's capacity to experience interest and enjoyment and with that, the impediment to emotional connection disappears. (In many cases, however, brief couples therapy is necessary to help repair any lasting damage done during the depressed partner's illness. Education about the biological effects of depression on the affect system goes a long way when repairing such damage.)

A brief note about the effect of antidepressant medication: I frequently encounter people who have the misconception that antidepressant medications are "uppers." They believe these medications force people to feel happy. Some even call them "happy pills." This is far from the truth. Effective antidepressants alter faulty brain biochemistry in such a way that the affect system returns to a normal state little by little. No one suddenly feels "happy" when starting an antidepressant. Instead, after a few weeks or sometimes longer, the unremitting distress begins to lessen and the ability to experience interest-excitement and enjoyment-joy gradually returns to normal. Once recovered, formerly depressed people no longer view the surrounding world through glasses coated with distress; that is, they cease misinterpreting everything that happens around them as distressing. In addition, successful treatment corrects a "glitched" affect system's tendency to over-amplify negative events and make them feel worse than they really are. The once-depressed person with a normalized affect system is now back in control of their emotions. The volume regulator for their emotions is back in their grasp and their ability to show interest in their partner, as well as to feel their partner's interest in them, returns.

Premenstrual syndrome is another biological condition with an impact on the affect system. Affect psychology–savvy women suffering from PMS report that three days or more before their menstrual flow begins, their levels of both distress affect and shame affect increase. While the intensity of this effect varies in each woman, I have yet to discover a single woman who says she enjoys these feelings. Instead, they report that not only is the effect unpleasant, but it is also embarrassing because they feel so much less in control of their emotions. The increase in distress causes them to cry more easily and feel more overwhelmed by things they usually handle without much difficulty. The increase in shame causes them to be very rejection sensitive. Things that others say or do, which normally would not bother them very much, are experienced as deeply hurtful.

Obviously, such distortions in the affect system, and the negative affect produced by them, impede emotional connection. Medicine can help. There is evidence that the sharp decrease in the hormones estrogen and progesterone preceding the onset of menses causes a decrease in the amount of the neurotransmitter serotonin in the brain. In addition, there occurs what is termed a "downregulation" of the receptors for serotonin—meaning they need more serotonin to work properly. Research has shown that the administration of serotonin-enhancing medications approximately ten days before the onset of menses reduces the intensity of the negative affect response. In other words, medicine can protect the affect system from the effects of the hormonal changes and reduce the impediment such effects have on emotional connection.

Though medicine can help ameliorate a host of other illnesses and physical conditions that cause difficulties for relationships, I will focus here on only one more—the now frequently diagnosed syndrome known as *attention deficit hyperactivity disorder*, or ADHD. One usually associates the diagnosis of ADHD with children. I encounter many adults, however, who in my opinion clearly suffer from untreated ADHD. ADHD is, technically speaking, a "condition" rather than an illness. An illness gets better or worse (varies over time), whereas a condition remains stable, i.e., once you have it, you will always have it at the same level of intensity.

The hallmark of this condition is distractibility. Distractibility triggers shame. The mechanism is exactly the same as the one I have delineated throughout this book—*impediment to positive affect*. People with ADHD experience frequent impediment to their interest-excitement and enjoyment-joy because even the most insignificant external stimulus—something others hardly notice—can completely distract them from what they are doing. Depending upon the severity of this distractibility, they experience everything from regular to very frequent impediment to ongoing interest and enjoyment. They suffer, therefore, from an excess of shame beginning with the onset of their ADHD, which is usually in early childhood. This means that from an early age they experience shame affect for reasons that have nothing to do with anything they have done or, for that matter, anything anyone else has done to them. It comes from a biologic glitch of their affect system.

The effect of excess shame on personality development is dramatic. A strong argument can be made that shame is the source of the "impulsivity" so characteristic of folks with ADHD. What is indisputable is that all of the major traits of ADHD—hyperactivity, impulsivity, and inattention—are behaviors unacceptable and difficult for most caregivers to manage. This becomes even more problematic when these children begin school and encounter classroom settings and teachers who demand quiet, attentive behavior. People with ADHD, therefore, are doubly shamed. Shame from their biology combines with shame about their behavior creating the need for very powerful defenses against shame. An examination of the Compass of Shame defenses ADHD sufferers necessarily develop will be the topic of a future book. For now, I will stick to the topic at hand and discuss the effects of ADHD on relationships. Suffice it to say that whether it is obvious to them and others or not, these are all people who develop very low self-esteem.

Distractibility is a clear-cut impediment to emotional connection. How could you not experience the shame emotions of rejection, frustration, and annoyance if your partner interrupts you in midsentence seventy-five times a day and blurts out something on a completely different topic? How could you not feel the shame emotions of distance and isolation if your partner never appears to be paying attention to you when you are talking? You would have to feel as if your partner is not interested in you, that other things are more important to her or him than you are. Couple these feelings in the unafflicted partner with shame-related behaviors in the ADHD partner, such as drug and alcohol abuse, sexual acting out, and impulsive attack other behaviors, and it is no wonder that multiple divorces are commonplace in people with ADHD.

As if this were not enough, ADHD afflicts its sufferers with a myriad of minor behavior problems that create distress in their partners and lead to emotional disconnection. They are constantly losing car keys, important documents, and even the prescriptions for medications that help their condition. Distractibility also affects their sense of time and their ability to complete tasks. They are almost always late to appointments, even for things they enjoy. They leave many tasks only partially completed because in mid task they become distracted by another task that needs doing and begin *it*, only to be distracted by yet another task and so on. This lifelong pattern makes it very difficult for them to develop a sense of how long it takes to do things. Needless to say, it always takes them longer to complete a task than they anticipate. It is as if they have a distorted sense of time.

(Old-fashioned psychiatric training taught me that a patient's lateness to an appointment was treatment "resistance," that it should be analyzed immediately as it was theorized to be "transference"—some sort of negative reaction to me, as if I were the patient's parent. Because psychoanalytic theorists of the time knew diddly-squat about shame, they had no clue that a focus on lateness, especially in people with ADHD, would only create more shame and transference reactions. As soon as I learned about shame, I stopped doing it. Instead, I attempt to reduce the shame ADHD patients have about their chronic lateness by announcing early in treatment that their sessions do not officially begin until twelve minutes after the scheduled start time—or whenever they heck they arrive. An interesting upshot of this strategy is that it improves the therapeutic alliance to the point where they can—without shame—analyze their own tendency to always do that "one last thing" before they leave for an appointment. This provides them with insight into their distorted sense of how long it takes them to complete tasks without the need to be defensive about it around me.)

Here, too, medicine can help. Stimulant medications that enhance the neurotransmitter dopamine in the brain produce dramatic reductions in distractibility for many with ADHD. The reduction of distractibility and the resulting improvement in the capacity to attend to one thing at a time come as a welcome relief for anyone with ADHD. They generally feel calmer and more in control of their emotions and their lives. Their shame level diminishes, and with it the need for Compass of Shame defenses diminishes. With the lessening of defensiveness, hyperactivity, inattentiveness, and impulsiveness comes a dramatic improvement in the ability to connect emotionally with their partners. Not surprisingly, their partners feel a great sense of relief, making them more open to dropping their own defensive postures. The process of reconnection after proper medical treatment proceeds more efficiently if they engage in couples therapy geared to education about the biologically induced shame effects of ADHD, about how Compass of Shame defenses have crept into their relationship, and about how to set in motion the missions presented in Chapters 8 and 9.

In summary, while I am a very strong advocate against the indiscriminate use of medication, I am also a very strong advocate in favor of using medication when needed. Many treatable illnesses either are or become impediments to emotional connection and trigger shame that can ruin intimate relationships. Prejudice against the use of medication is widespread in Western culture. My guess is that there would be a significant drop in the rate of divorce with the proper use of medication in many situations. Should we be prejudiced against the use of medication to save marriages? In the wake of the destructive power of divorce in married life, and its negative effect on any children involved, I vote no. At the very least, everyone should be given the chance to feel good enough to practice the art of intimacy in loving, caring ways.

APPENDIX I

A PRIMER OF AFFECT PSYCHOLOGY

Introduction

The purpose of this primer is to introduce the reader to the work of Silvan S. Tomkins. Tomkins dedicated his life to developing a new, more comprehensive understanding of the biological and evolutionary roots of human motivation. He wanted to establish a more accurate picture of personality, something he called Human Being Theory. Tomkins's formal educational background included the study of playwriting, philosophy, and psychology. It is clear from reading the four volumes of his magnum opus, *Affect Imagery Consciousness*, that he was also well-versed in many other areas, including anatomy, Darwinian evolution, history, literature, religion, and artificial intelligence, all of which he pursued to answer the question: "What do human beings really want?"

My introduction to Tomkins's theories took place in the early 1980s when I first read volumes I and II of *Affect Imagery Consciousness* (from here on abbreviated as AIC). These two volumes were first published in 1962 and 1963. My motivation for reading them came from my colleague Donald L. Nathanson, M.D., whose excitement at discovering Tomkins's ideas was contagious. Both of us realized that in spite of our extensive psychiatric training, there was something missing in the way we conceptualized human motivation. Our joint excitement, however, was soon reduced by the shame we experienced reading AIC. It was difficult going at first, both because Tomkins's dense writing style was difficult to penetrate and because his theories presented a major paradigm shift regarding human motivation. Ultimately, we formed a study group with several other colleagues, and the collegial atmosphere proved to be an excellent means to share the reading with greater understanding and thereby reduce our shame, keeping alive our interest in learning more. For me, the result was a transformation in the way I see human motivation, my own included, and therefore in the way I work with my patients.

To make your work easier, I have for the most part limited this primer to a moderately superficial presentation of the component of Tomkins's work best learned first—affect psychology. This is the logical place to start because it is the most basic building block of his theory of human motivation and personality formation. It is important to keep in mind that affect psychology is a complete shift from the way we usually think of emotion. What you learned either formally through education or informally by word-of-mouth are the current culturally determined beliefs about human emotion and motivation that are missing vital pieces of information. As a result, while what follows should seem logical to you, it may also seem a bit strange at first, and you may experience some shame trying to understand it. I have tried very hard to minimize any negative affect triggered by this learning experience, but the reality is that paradigm shifts seldom come easily to any of us.

I have written this primer in the style of the verbal presentation I make to many of my patients in their early sessions once we have established a goal for therapy. It is my belief that we are very much what we feel, that we live primarily in the affect of the moment, and that it is impossible to know the self without knowing what we feel, accurately and immediately.

My patients tell me that although I have given them entirely too much information about affect psychology in too short a time, they think they understand. But in truth, we spend the rest of our time together on a journey toward solidifying that understanding. I dedicate this work to them for the intense interest-excitement they have triggered in me by permitting me to travel with them in their journey toward better self-understanding. I hope you, too, find interest-excitement in reading the following pages, and that your understanding of what you and those around you "really want" is enhanced.

Beginnings

There is no best place to begin any description of affect psychology. Nor do I intend to start with a simple definition of "affect." You will better understand affect when you can see it in the overall context of its general purpose. However, before going there, it is worth noting that an affect is a biological event, a normal part of the everyday functioning of our central nervous system (CNS). An affect is, in some respects, like a normal knee-jerk reflex. If one applies the proper stimulus to the patellar tendon—a tap with a small hammer—in just the right place with just the right amount of force, the lower leg will jerk upwards. Similarly, if the CNS receives a proper stimulus, an affect is triggered. How this takes place will become clear later on, but for now, please do not think of an affect as some kind of mysterious psychological event. It is not. It is simply a normal part of brain functioning that has evolved in our species for a specific purpose. It is so much a part of everyday life that you seldom think about it and often do not even recognize its presence.

Tomkins paid a great deal of attention to the work of the evolutionist Charles Darwin. Once he had recognized that our CNS contains a system comprised of nine affects, his inquiring mind needed to know why we *have* affects and what function they serve. He turned to Darwin's work, especially concerning the universal nature of facial responses. Darwin believed that it was no accident, for instance, that when in the midst of **enjoyment**, all peoples, regardless of race or place, smile the same way. (The bold italicized words are my way of introducing several of the affects before I present them more formally. I want you to begin to think of them as a normal, everyday part of life and not as some mysterious piece of psychobabble.) Since Tomkins perceived the face to be an integral part of the affect system, he looked to evolution for an explanation as to why our species needed an affect system.

His conclusion was that the affect system evolved to solve a problem that threatened survival. The problem was *stimulus confusion*. Imagine that in the very earliest stages of humans' emergence, especially after we developed the ability to move significant distances on foot, we had many, if not all, of our senses intact. By this point in our evolution, it is likely that we could at least see, hear, smell, taste, and feel things by touch. This meant that at each instant in time, the primitive brain would have been receiving a great deal of information from and about the surrounding world. In addition—and this is still true today—the human brain lacked the capacity to be consciously aware of large amounts of stimuli simultaneously. Tomkins called this a *limited channel of consciousness*.

With this limited consciousness and so many stimuli hitting us all at once, how could we sort it out rapidly? Survival demanded that we be able to attend immediately to the most significant events. I imagine it as being comparable to walking in a large mall during the holiday season with hundreds of people rushing around and bumping into you, loud music blaring, the smells of many things cooking, gaudy decorations dangling from the ceiling, lights flashing in all the stores. The stimulus overload makes it so difficult to concentrate that one could easily forget what they wanted to buy. (I've sometimes come home with a bunch of stuff, none of which I really wanted or needed, and without the right present for my wife.)

Tomkins surmised that the affect system evolved as a normal brain function to reduce confusion from this kind of stimulus overload. He proposed that in order for us to become conscious of any stimulus, it must first activate the affect system. I will detail how this happens later. The conclusion he derived from this proposal is that stimuli that do **not** trigger an affect do **not** enter into our conscious awareness! This conceptualization is a radical departure from most psychological theories of emotional functioning. In brief, most prior theories postulate that some form of learning must take place before you have feelings about something. Tomkins studied children—you can do this yourself by observing very young babies—and saw affect on their faces from the moment of birth. The most obvious is the affect *distress*, visible on the face and in the cry of all normal newborns as they emerge from the birth canal. Obviously, no learning has occurred that would cause an infant to view its world as distressing. Instead, Tomkins said, the affect of distress is an innate, inborn response to the stimulus conditions that act upon the baby.

The bottom line of Tomkins's observations is that conscious awareness of anything happens **only** with the triggering of an affect. Since only one affect can be triggered at a time, any stimulus that triggers an affect is the only stimulus we can be aware of at that instant. If, for instance, my writing here is sufficiently clear and entertaining, then it will trigger in you the affect of *interest*. As long as your interest is maintained, it will be easier for you to sort out other sights and sounds in the environment and focus on what you are reading. If a more powerful stimulus such as an earthquake occurs, then that will trigger *fear* in you, and your entire focus and attention will center on protecting yourself.

The evolutionary significance of the affect system, then, is to *simplify* things by directing attention to one stimulus at a time. With this simplifying mechanism in place, the problem of stimulus confusion is eased. As suggested in the above example, this is especially important if that thing poses a danger to existence. The sight of a car careening at you from the other side of the street or a lion charging at you through the jungle gains immediate attention. You do not have to *think* about it. The careening car or charging lion triggers fear affect, just like the reflex hammer on the knee triggers the knee jerk. How many times have you heard someone say about a crisis, "I didn't think, I just reacted"? This is one of the characteristics of all nine of the affects, not just fear. You do not "think" about any of them, they are triggered by stimulus conditions and just happen. Overall, it is very likely that the human species would have become extinct if we had not developed an affect system. It is no wonder then that Tomkins believed the affect system to be a critical element in human motivational systems. I think of the affect system as being like a lens between conscious awareness and the world around us: everything must pass through the lens before we become aware of it.

Brain Systems

One way to think about our CNS is to conceptualize it based on the various functions it performs. It is somewhat artificial to do this, since normally functioning brains have all systems working simultaneously in concert with one another. However, it will make it easier to understand the special nature and functions of the affect system if we contrast it with the other functional brain systems. Furthermore, historically there has been disagreement among psychological theorists as to which system is THE primary motivator of human behavior. The four parts worthy of the greatest consideration are the Drive System, the Pain System, the Cognitive System, and the Affect System. (Keep in mind that when I use the word *system*, I am referring to brain "function" and not necessarily to any specific area in the brain.)

The Pain System

Our pain system operates very much like a subroutine running in a computer. It is poised in the background ready to react whenever there is a need. For instance, if a pin sticks into your leg, the nerve endings from that spot send a signal to the brain. You feel pain almost instantaneously and are motivated to locate the spot where it hurts and remove the pin. After rubbing the spot for a moment or two, the pain goes away. As soon as it is gone, the pain system retreats into the background. The pain system, therefore, is a motivator. It motivates for very specific events that take place within our bodies. Through memory and learning, we are further motivated to avoid things that cause us physical pain. As adults, having learned what hurts, our avoidance of those things becomes automatic. We do not have to think about it very much, and we can trust the pain system to let us know when we've made a mistake.

As a motivator for the more meaningful things in our life, like career and relationship choices, the pain system is seldom very important because it is so limited. Also, it is often the case that the affect system and the emotions it leads to override motivational messages from the pain system. For instance, we have all heard dramatic stories like the one about the severely wounded soldier who should be crippled by intense pain. Instead, when his buddy in the foxhole beside him is killed, his *rage* is so great, it overrides his pain and he attacks the enemy who killed his friend. Likewise, there are many stories of parents who ignore their own pain and run into burning buildings willing to suffer horrendous burns because of their fear for their beloved children.

Less dramatic is the fact of everyday life that we have many aches and pains all the time, and we ignore them because of affect. We have all "forgotten" about toothaches or stomachaches or joint pain because something we were doing was of great interest or caused fear or distress. Obviously, as powerful as the pain system can be, the affect system is often much more motivating.

The Drive System

This system of brain functions deals with things going into and out of our bodies on a periodic basis. The basic drives are hunger, defecation, urination, breathing, and sexuality. Those who are familiar with the work of Sigmund Freud know this as the system he postulated as having the greatest motivational power, especially sexual drive. Affect psychologists do not agree. They believe that drives give us information as to where and when there is a need, but they are not especially motivating. Here are some examples.

Periodically, hunger drive appears and signals us that we are hungry or thirsty in the stomach or mouth—the where and when information. However, think about how often we ignore this information. If you have a strong interest in something you are doing, you may ignore hunger signals for many hours. Many people while experiencing fear are unable to eat until the fear goes away. The opposite thing can happen if somebody offers us a particularly interesting-looking preparation of food and we eat even though we are not hungry. Sometimes we eat because we are in distress and it feels as if eating will provide relief. We can also ignore for long periods signals that we need to urinate or defecate if engaged in interesting activities. This changes when activation of the pain system triggers sufficient distress to motivate us to head for the bathroom.

Breathing is an interesting drive that, for the most part, we ignore until something happens to impede it. The fear that arises when that happens is highly motivating. Currently, we do not understand well the connection between fear and breathing, but some researchers theorize that panic disorder is the result of a defect in the respiratory mechanism in the brain.

What about sex drive as a motivator? It certainly gives information about a need in the genitals, but it, too, is subject to the motivating forces of the affect system. Imagine being at the height of sexual excitement with your partner only to have someone enter the room and point a gun at your head. Fear immediately shuts off any interest in sex. Likewise, if one's partner says something that triggers **shame** ("Is that as big it gets?" or "Is that cellulite on your legs?"), sexuality becomes the farthest thing from your mind.

I could quote many more examples of how affects control motivation related to the drives. Hopefully, these few examples provide you with a feel for the message: **The drives give us information about something we need and the place where we need it, but it is the affects that motivate us to do something about that information.**

The Cognitive System

This is the system in our brains that handles a wide variety of things such as 1 + 1 = 2, the wild imagination involved in the writing of science fiction, the beauty of a landscape, and the love of country. It is vital for memory recall and problem solving. It both *acquires* raw data and *transforms* it into understanding and knowledge.

I began this section on brain systems with the idea that we can describe the brain by dividing it into separate functions. While it may be clear that the function of the affect system is more powerfully motivating than the pain and drive functions, we cannot say the same of the cognitive system. Tomkins's genius was that he was able to unpack the complexity of human behavior down to its basic motivational roots. To do so, he had to temporarily ignore the cognitive system and draw all attention to the motivational significance of the affect system, even though he certainly understood that the two do not function as completely separate systems in normal brains. They really work hand in hand.

Tomkins postulated that the purely "rational" understanding or knowledge of something by cognitive processes is not motivating without affect. Likewise, the purely "emotional" originating from within the affect system operates in the dark without cognition. From the point of view of survival of the species, a real separation in the functioning of these two systems would be a disaster. For example, the fear triggered (by a biologic mechanism that will soon be explained) when a car is spotted heading right at you would not be acted on properly if you did not have knowledge about the possible consequences of not moving out of the way. You might simply stand there frozen in terror. For the same reason, the knowledge that the car is coming at you is useless until fear motivates you to move. Otherwise, you might stand there wondering about the paint job or the design of the front bumper. The bottom line is that the cognitive system and affect system have an open channel to one another. They operate together even though they have different functions.

The Affect System

The technical details of the affect system fill about 1400 of the most densely detailed pages one can imagine. In this primer, I have intentionally omitted most of these details in an attempt to avoid both confusion and the need to write another 1400 pages. For those who wish to understand the full breadth and depth of Tomkins's description of the affect system, you will have to read his work directly. (If you do, I suggest you find several other scholarly friends and colleagues and start a study group. It is difficult and often confounding work plowing through the four volumes of *Affect Imagery Consciousness*, but the reward, in my opinion, is great.)

I have already mentioned that Tomkins conceptualized the affect system as an evolutionary event to protect our species from the dangers of stimulus overload on the brain. The affect system simplifies things by permitting only one stimulus at a time to enter consciousness. The best analogy I have heard to describe this comes from the lectures of my colleague Don Nathanson. To expand his analogy a bit, imagine yourself in a large theater. There is frenetic action taking place on an almost-dark stage with a very large cast of characters, all speaking simultaneously. The scene is confusing and unintelligible. It is virtually impossible to ascertain the most salient features of the show. Now imagine that there is a bank of nine powerful spotlight/sound devices. Only one of these devices can be on at a time, and each one can go on and off in rapid succession if necessary. Imagine next that when a **special signal** is given, a spotlight/sound device points directly at one actor and everything else on the stage goes completely dark. As soon as the spotlight makes the actor highly visible, his microphone turns on and all the other microphones are muted. That one actor is now seen and heard clearly. This simplifies your task of following the plot because the action of the spotlight/sound device narrows your focus to one thing (one stimulus) at a time. In this analogy, each of the spotlight/sound devices represents an affect and the **special signal** represents the **stimulus condition** for that affect.

The mechanics of how the affect system creates focus on one stimulus at a time require a bit of explaining. When the sensory system—eyes and ears in the above analogy—detects a stimulus that meets certain criteria (the details of which are beyond the scope of this primer), it transmits information to the face and then back to the brain. During this process, the affects **amplify** the stimulus. This amplification causes sufficient brain activity to trigger conscious awareness of and focus upon that stimulus alone. In the spotlight/sound device analogy, the intensification of the light on a single actor and the turning up of his microphone represent the process of amplification.

I have gone into this brief description of the mechanics of affect amplification to draw attention to the significance of the **face** for affect psychology. For those with a strong interest in the science of the brain, I have included below two somewhat strange-looking diagrams of the sensory and motor representations of the human body in the cerebral cortex. (These diagrams are called the homunculus, a word that comes from Latin and means "little man." I copied them from the following url: https://nahsanatomy.wikispaces.com/Nervous+system; unfortunately, that website does not include any information about the creator of this interesting version of the homunculus.) What these diagrams show is that the face has a greater representation in the brain than any other part of the body with the possible exception of the hand. This means that the information going back and forth between the face and the brain is so important that evolution granted the face a very large share of its cortical function. Charles Darwin was obviously on the right track paying so much attention to the facial expression of emotion among the different peoples of the world.

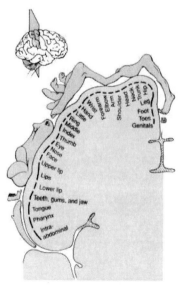

(a) Somatosensory cortex in right cerebral hemisphere

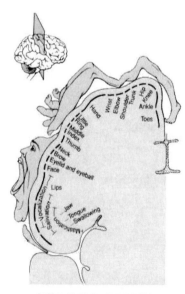

(b) Motor cortex in right cerebral hemisphere

Following Darwin's lead, Tomkins carried out many detailed studies of the face, including that of his infant son, Mark. He came to realize that each of the nine affects has a distinct facial pattern. As we turn now to a description of the individual affects, the facial pattern of each will become an important way for you to begin to distinguish one affect from another. If you want to get an even clearer understanding of affect, I encourage you to study the faces of people you know, and even your own face in the mirror. A number of my patients, especially those with difficulty recognizing their own affect, have had remarkable success increasing awareness of affect by studying their faces in the mirror.

Affects come in three basic flavors—positive, neutral, or negative. *Positive* affects are *inherently rewarding*, and we are motivated to do things to have them continue or get them back if they happen to be blocked. *Negative* affects are *inherently punishing*, and we are motivated to do things to get rid of them and avoid things that will arouse them. The one neutral affect is just that—neutral—it does not motivate us to do much of anything. The nine affects—listed in their positive, negative, or neutral categories—are as follows:

POSITIVE AFFECTS:	INTEREST-EXCITEMENT
	ENJOYMENT-JOY
NEUTRAL AFFECT:	SURPRISE-STARTLE
NEGATIVE AFFECTS:	FEAR-TERROR
	DISTRESS-ANGUISH
	ANGER-RAGE
	DISGUST
	DISSMELL
	SHAME-HUMILIATION

As you can see, Tomkins used common everyday words to name the affects, with the exception of the made-up word *dissmell*. He considered all but two as being somewhat different in their upper and lower range of intensity. Rage, for instance, is clearly not simple anger, but the difference is only one of intensity, whereas mild disgust and intense disgust still feel pretty much like disgust.

While I have yet to define the word "affect," I hope that by now its general meaning is beginning to emerge. Here is a distinction that should help: When those of us who work with affect psychology say someone has a **feeling**, we mean that person has become aware of a **biological response**; in other words, they have become aware of their **affect**. Affects and the resulting feelings are inborn parts of our biology. We all have the *same nine affects*. We all "know" what fear, shame, joy, anger, or any of the rest feel like because we have all experienced them.

From the time we are born, however, our environment begins to alter our innate affective responses into **emotions**. Every family in every culture handles affect differently. Anger in one family will be encouraged and in another suppressed. Some families treat the more vulnerable affects like fear, shame, or distress with compassion; while others scorn them as weaknesses with responses like "Big boys don't cry" or "If you don't stop crying, I'll give you something to really cry about." Emotion, therefore, is not innate like affect. Instead, it is learned. (Tomkins used the term **script** to describe the complex things that happen during such learning.) Emotion is the result of our affective biography. It develops uniquely in each of us, scripted from our life experience with our affects, the responses of others to our affects, and our observations of the affects of those around us. As a result, we are all *different emotionally*. One person's anger scripts may involve ranting, raving, and cursing like a sailor, while another person, just as angry, might simply raise an eyebrow. The bottom line is that **affect** is **biology** and **emotion** is **biology mixed with biography**.

Another concept is worth considering before tackling each of the nine affects in detail. It is common today to compare our brains to computers. From a functional standpoint, our brain is a "device" that gathers, analyzes, and stores **information**. The affect system is critical to this process. One way to think about the affect system is that its job is to simplify the task of becoming aware of important information. It sounds a bit strange, but an affect is really information about information. Tomkins postulated that the evolution of the affect system followed the pattern of the information (stimuli) around us. As a result, each affect mimics—or is an analog of—the pattern of the stimulus that triggers it. Understanding these patterns is vital to understanding affect psychology.

When the CNS receives a stimulus, the instantaneous response of the brain can only be in one of three patterns. As the graph below illustrates, there can be an increase, a decrease, or some level of a steady-state pattern of brain activity. (This is another oversimplification; you can find more details in *AIC* Vol. 1, pages 250–258.)

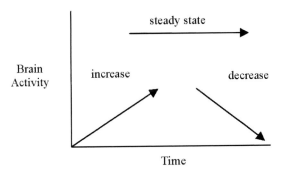

Because the similarity of the patterns of stimulus and affect to one another is important to understanding how affects come about, the discussion of the details of the individual affects will follow the pattern of these patterns. Also included will be a description and picture of each affect's facial expression. There are thousands of words in our everyday language for feelings and emotions. Once one has a clear grasp of affect psychology, one can reduce those thousands of common words to just nine—the innate affects delineated by Tomkins. The ability to do this greatly simplifies the process of figuring out emotional motivations in yourself and in others.

Increasing Rate of Brain Activity

Interest-Excitement
Tomkins postulated that there must be an "ideal" rate of increase in brain activity produced by certain stimuli. This rate of increasing activity is fast enough for us to notice, but not so fast as to be unpleasant. The affect triggered by any stimulus pattern producing this pattern of brain activity he named *interest-excitement*. Interest-excitement is a POSITIVE affect and is inherently rewarding. Here is the graph of this pattern:
Thousands of stimuli in daily life trigger mild interest. Even though the affect interest frequently directs attention from one task to the next, we seldom think about it unless it is triggered at the more intense end of the range—excitement. The repeated occurrence of interest in one's lifetime causes people to become more or less unaware of its presence when it is only mild interest. (This lack of awareness is the reason most researchers have completely ignored this very important affect for centuries.) Please keep in mind that each time a stimulus triggers an affect, the

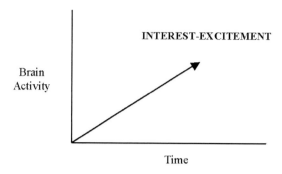

brain is immediately ready for the next affect. As a result, an innate affect lasts only milliseconds. To go back to the spotlight/sound device analogy: affects being triggered are like the spotlight/sound devices going on and off very quickly.

When *interest-excitement* is triggered, *the eyebrows turn down and the face has a "track, look, and listen" appearance.* The affects are all visible on the face virtually from birth. The picture on the left is of my granddaughter Maddy. She is 22 days old and has had mild interest triggered. The picture on the right is of my granddaughter Katie at age 23 months, exhibiting the more intense form of this affect. She is very excited when, as she says, "run so fast."

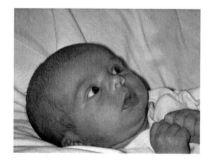 

Novelty is the primary *stimulus condition* that triggers interest-excitement.

Fear-Terror
When a stimulus has a pattern of too rapid an increase in brain activity—that is, when too much is happening too fast—the affect *fear-terror* is triggered. Fear-terror is the most toxic of the NEGATIVE affects. It is inherently punishing, and we are motivated to stop it as quickly as pos-

sible. As you can see in the graph below, the rate at which brain activity increases when a fear-terror stimulus is present is faster than when a stimulus triggering interest-excitement is involved. The brain is clearly receiving two different patterns of information that distinguish these two affects from one another.

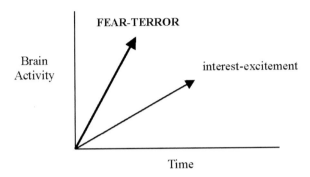

One of the features of the affect system is that it does not care what the actual stimulus is; it only responds to the pattern of the stimulus. For instance, a lion at the zoo is something we do not see very often. In such a setting, it is a novel stimulus and triggers interest-excitement. The same lion charging at us would trigger fear-terror because the stimulus pattern has changed. Note that anything and everything that triggers the stimulus pattern above will trigger fear-terror whether it is a charging lion, a car heading right for us, the howling winds of a hurricane, a robber pointing a gun at us, etc. In other words, the affect system is a very general system. It responds to the pattern of a stimulus without regard to the cause of the pattern.

You can see an interesting point about interest-excitement and fear-terror by studying the graph again. If we assume that the position of lines I have drawn represents only one set of stimulus conditions, then it is possible in other situations that the two might be very close together. This explains something we have all experienced: being afraid of something we were very excited about or, put another way, feeling excitement about something that we fear.

In the facial display of *fear-terror, the eyes become wide open and frozen. The face gets pale, cold, and sweaty, and the hair, especially on the back of the neck, becomes erect.* Here is a picture of my grandson Collin on his third birthday. To celebrate, his mother has just ignited a little sparkler. She thought he would enjoy it, but, as you can see, he is so afraid that the fear has disrupted his interest in both his ice cream cone and his trains (and that is remarkable because he is very, very interested in his trains).

While his interest in ice cream and trains returned shortly after the sparkler burned out, this story calls to mind an important aspect of what Tomkins called **affect dynamics**. *Stimuli that trigger negative affect almost always prevail over stimuli that trigger positive affect.* In this instance, the affect fear-terror triggered by the sparkler overrode his interest-excitement in food or toys and focused him on the feared object. The survival value of this dynamic is obvious. Stimulus conditions where too much is happening too fast are much more likely to be a danger to us than most other stimulus conditions. However, stimulus conditions that trigger distress-anguish, anger-rage, shame-humiliation, disgust, and dissmell, while less dangerous than fear-terror, still have an element of danger to them. Therefore, it is usually prudent to turn away from interesting or enjoyable things to deal with the cause of the danger. That the affect system evolved in this manner clearly provided a survival advantage for our species.

Surprise-Startle

This is the third and last of the innate affects triggered by stimuli that produce a pattern of *increasing* brain activity. This is also the only NEUTRAL affect. Its pattern is the same as that of a sound wave created by a gunshot or a clap of thunder. There is a rapid increase then a rapid decrease of brain activity.

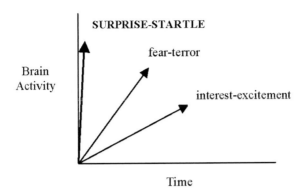

I cheated a bit in the above graph and drew only a single line going up to show the pattern of brain activity representing the pattern of surprise-startle. The line should go straight up and down, but that would be more difficult to show in this graphic format. *Surprise-startle* is a neutral affect that once triggered *resets* everything. It creates immediate attention to the triggering stimulus and clears away all else from consciousness. It is like the reset button on a computer.

With *surprise-startle, the eyebrows go up, the eyes blink, and the mouth gets an O shape.* Here is Collin at six weeks. The camera caught his facial expression just after he had blinked. The eyes are still wide open and the mouth in the O shape.

Look carefully at his face and notice that he does not seem either happy or unhappy. Surprise-startle is a neutral affect from which another affect quickly follows. For instance, imagine walking down a dark hallway at night and someone unexpectedly taps you on the shoulder. After a startle response of very brief duration, you would more than likely feel fear-terror. If the person were someone you knew, you would probably then get angry and yell, "What are you doing? You scared me to death!"

Positive affect can also follow surprise-startle. Years ago, I was watching the annual Wimbledon tennis tournament from the All England Club on TV. There was a rain delay and the camera panned back to show the entire upper tier of the stadium filled with spectators. Suddenly there was a flash of lightning and a clap of thunder very close to the stadium. As one, the crowd startled, immediately after which they all looked around and began to laugh. (In affect terms, after the intense startle, they had a sudden decrease in brain activity triggering the innate affect enjoyment-joy, the details of which I will describe later.) The point is that while surprise-startle is a neutral affect that clears consciousness in order to rapidly direct attention to the triggering stimulus, it is usually soon followed by another affect.

Steady-State Brain Activity

Distress-Anguish
This NEGATIVE affect is *inherently punishing* and triggered by any stimulus that has a pattern that is too dense for too long.

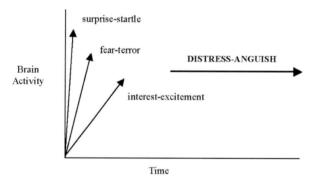

The above graph represents the steady-state nature of the pattern of brain activity that characterizes **distress-anguish**. (To all scientists and mathematicians: Pay no attention to the various levels shown in any of my graphs. I am presenting the graphs to represent Tomkins's concept of the innate activators of affect. To date, I know of no experimental data from research specifically directed toward measuring the levels of CNS activity associated with the affects.)

Whenever there is an above-optimal, steady-state pattern of stimulus density, distress-anguish occurs. What kinds of things might create such a pattern? Recently, there was road work going on outside of my office, which is located no more than forty or fifty feet from the road. There were many instances when the sound from the heavy equipment was loud and constant. As you can imagine, this made it difficult to hear. My patients and I had to talk louder and concentrate harder to make ourselves understood. My patients and I experienced distress-anguish during those instances when the steady-state, intense noise was at its loudest. (It is a poor advertisement for psychiatry when the patient feels *more* distress in the office rather than having distress relieved! Fortunately, everyone was very understanding.)

Noise is far from the only dense, steady-state stimulus that triggers distress-anguish. Much of what we do in our daily work provides steady-state stimulus density, especially when one must work continually throughout the day and the work is never completely finished. Other steady-state stimuli include such things as the need to urinate while stuck in traffic, the honking horns and stop-and-go nature of traffic at rush hour, constant thoughts of all we have to do on a busy day or during exam week, the persistent needs and demands of small children, the complaints of retail customers, and any condition or disease that causes chronic pain. The list could go on and on, but by now I hope you have the idea of what I mean by a steady-state, above-optimal stimulus of a dense nature.

The facial response indicative of *distress-anguish* includes *crying, tears, arching of the eyebrows, a mouth with turned-down corners, and rhythmic sobbing.* The next picture is of Maddy when she was about two weeks old. It is not a perfect picture of distress-anguish because I seldom wait around looking for the perfect face of any negative affect before picking her up, although her grandmother usually beats me to it. However, you can see the arching of the eyebrows and can assume from the pose that she was in distress and crying.

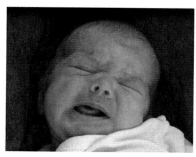

This might be a good time to make use of a mirror to study your own affect. With the mirror in front of you, try turning down the corners of your mouth and push your eyebrows together letting your forehead wrinkle as you do. You will feel your eyes shut partially. Did you notice that even if you were interested in this exercise, it did not feel good? Tomkins did a number of experiments asking subjects to answer a meaningless questionnaire after having them put their faces into this pose. When they were finished, he asked them what they thought about the questionnaire. Most said that, although they could not put their finger on exactly why, there was something distressing about the questions. I have had actors tell me that in order to get into the mood called for by a scene, they will often set their face first to get the mood started.

Affect psychologists have a problem with the way most people use the word "depression," especially those who conceive of depression as a disease. Instead, we think of depression as a syndrome with symptoms that often include fear, distress, anger, and shame, as well as reductions in the ability to experience interest and enjoyment. Brain research into causes and treatments for affect disorders would be remarkably more proficient were it informed by Tomkins's affect psychology insights. What the term depression really means is that someone suffering from it is experiencing *distress-anguish*. At lower levels of intensity, one would say that the person is feeling sad. At the higher levels, they are depressed. Because distress-anguish is triggered by any stimulus that is dense and steady-state in nature, it follows that chronic fear or chronic shame can trigger it. Treating "depression" is ineffective in such situations unless one addresses the fear and shame involved.

Anger-Rage

This NEGATIVE affect is *inherently punishing* and triggered by stimuli that have a pattern that is steady-state but even more dense and above-optimal than those that trigger distress-anguish.

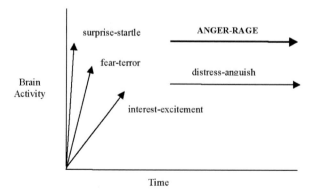

The line representing anger-rage in the graph indicates that stimuli triggering it have a pattern that is denser than that of distress-anguish. Such stimuli create a level of brain activity that is too much. Anger-rage is, therefore, the affect of overload. Imagine being stuck in heavy stop-and-go traffic on the way to work, with horns honking, with worry building that you are going to be late for an appointment, with people calling your cell phone wondering where you are and asking questions that you can only answer from your desk. The very next thing that happens will probably trigger anger, not because you are an "angry" person, but because the stimulus density is too great.

With tongue in cheek, I suggest in lectures that if I locked most folks in a room filled with very loud and purposely unintelligible rap music, almost all of them would soon become angry and pound on the door demanding to be let out. This is not because they are angry people. It is simply a matter that the overly dense pattern of the stimulus has triggered their anger-rage. (During one lecture a woman said, "But I like rap music." I replied that perhaps if I played Sinatra instead, it might have the same effect.)

The important point here is that the triggering of any affect occurs as a reflex. If stimulus conditions create an overly dense, steady-state pattern in someone's brain, the result will always be the triggering of anger-rage. It matters not who the person is or what the actual stimulus is. We can alter stimulus conditions, but once we experience a particular stimulus condition, a specific affect is going to be triggered. We cannot stop the triggering of that affect any more than we can stop our knee from jerking when the reflex hammer hits the right spot on the tendon. It is for this reason that I believe the widely held notion that certain people are "angry" people is inadequate and better explained once one has a working knowledge of affect psychology. While it is true that there are people who become angry much more easily and quickly than others, this is often because something has caused in them a chronically high level of distress-anguish. Therefore, it only takes minor additional stimuli, things that would never trigger anger in someone with normal levels of distress-anguish, to trigger their anger. These are people we often think of as having a "short fuse."

One finds a common example of this phenomenon in many people diagnosed with "depression." Textbooks list "irritability" as one of the classic symptoms of depression. In other words, anger-rage is triggered in them easily and often. As noted in my discussion of distress-anguish, so-called depressed people have a chronically high level of distress-anguish. Below is a graphic representation of why anger is easily triggered in someone with high levels of distress. The shorter dotted line in the graph on the right implies that a smaller amount of additional brain activity is necessary before anger-rage is triggered. That is, little things can trigger angry very easily.

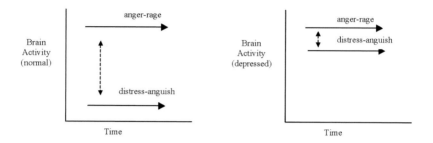

The facial display of *anger-rage* is one we all recognize. *The face becomes red, accompanied by a frown and a clenched jaw.* A colleague took this picture of her son when he was less than two months old:

Unfortunately (or fortunately), I have no pictures of my grandchildren that demonstrate infant anger-rage. And now they are too old for me to capture the pure affect because they are so used to their grandfather pointing a camera at them, they quickly pose when they see it. However, they are also at an age where, even if I did catch them in a moment of anger, their faces would probably not show the "pure" affect of anger-rage. All children begin modifying their expression of innate affect very early in life. These changes are a part of what Tomkins called "script" formation. Scripts are partly biology and partly a process of learning, especially learning by observation of how the adults in the child's life express affect and respond to his expression of affect. Script formation leads to what I earlier defined as "emotion." Scripts are a mechanism we use to simplify experience and our responses to it. It is beyond the scope of this current description of the affects to delve further into the fascinating and important realm of scripts. However, scripts can complicate the detection of affect. For instance, anger is difficult to ascertain in a person who learned to quietly clench his fists when angry, as opposed to a younger Collin who used to hurl himself on the floor and scream in rage.

Decreasing Rate of Brain Activity

Enjoyment-Joy
It may seem strange at first to think of brain activity decreasing, but look at the graph below and the position of the line representing enjoyment-joy.

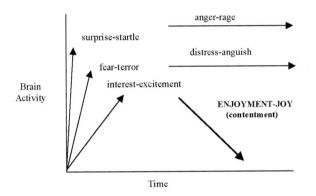

Enjoyment-joy is a POSITIVE affect that is *inherently rewarding* and triggered by any decreasing stimulus pattern that causes an analogous decreasing pattern of brain activity. As you may have already guessed from looking at the graph, some above-zero level of brain activity must be taking place before a stimulus can trigger enjoyment-joy. For example, you get home after being stuck in traffic for several hours with the pressing need to urinate having been with you the entire time. Needless to say, you are experiencing the steady-state brain activity of distress-anguish. Emptying your bladder ends your distress and causes a decrease in brain activity that triggers enjoyment-joy or contentment.

Here is another example. Someone begins telling you a joke. If you have never heard this joke before, in other words only if it is novel (the primary stimulus condition for interest-excitement), your brain begins to work to try to follow where the jokester is heading. This creates an increasing level of brain activity and triggers interest-excitement. Once he delivers the punch line and you "get" the joke, there is a split second of surprise-startle, and then no more need to think about it. The subsequent decreasing level of activity triggers enjoyment-joy. If there is a very rapid decrease in activity, usually associated with the cleverest jokes, then the laughter of joy follows. If the joke is simpler, like a pun, for instance, there is a less steep decrease and you experience something more like the amusement of enjoyment. As these two examples indicate, another affect that can be either positive or negative always precedes *enjoyment-joy*.

The face of *enjoyment-joy* is a pleasure and characterized by *smiling and a widening up and out of the lips*. I have thousands of pictures of my grandchildren experiencing enjoyment-joy. Reluctantly, I include only two: one of Maddy at age 2 ½ months (left) and Louisa at five months:

Even though I have seen these pictures many times, I cannot help but smile every time I see them. Did you smile, too? It is not just because they are so beautiful—the opinion of the grandfather—but we smile because *affect is contagious*. I have heard it said that the ability to smile between the ages of six and eight weeks saves the life of each child. Up until that time, the task of the caregiver is primarily one of responding to cries of distress-anguish that trigger distress-anguish in the caregiver. Before six to eight weeks, the reward one receives for taking care of whatever is causing distress-anguish in the baby is that the baby, when relieved of hunger, wetness, or whatever else might have triggered distress, has a decreasing rate of brain activity that triggers enjoyment-joy (contentment). This acts to relieve distress-anguish in the caregiver and therefore triggers enjoyment-joy (contentment) in the caregiver. However, this can be short-lived if the caregiver is exhausted, because exhaustion is a steady-state stimulus that triggers distress-anguish.

But once the infant's CNS matures sufficiently to allow for a full-fledged smile when enjoyment-joy is triggered, the reward for anyone who sees the smile is that, because of affect contagion, they also experience enjoyment-joy. This is so rewarding it promotes interest-excitement in seeing the baby smile again and again. As a result, people do all kinds of funny, interesting things—such as "making faces" at the baby or playing peekaboo—in order to repeat the experience. This is the starting point of what I call the second "social" script. If one were to graph this sequence, both the baby and the face-making adult would have a pattern like this:

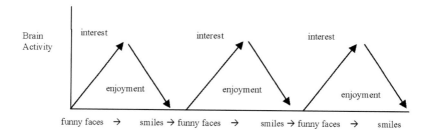

The alternating of interest-excitement and enjoyment-joy is the basis of the most pleasurable times in our lives. A technical note: It is important to remember that an innate affect, once triggered, only lasts for a brief period. (The spotlights flick on and off rapidly.) Therefore, for a "pleasurable time" to last, some stimulus condition that continually retriggers interest-excitement must be present. In the caregiver–infant sequence, the stimulus is the caregiver's ongoing interest in the baby that eventually scripts the baby's interest in the caregiver. I call this a "social" script because it instills in the child an interest in people that is distinctly interpersonal. If successful—and except for extremely unfortunate circumstances, it usually is—the child will have a script that makes her interested in positive (inherently rewarding) relationships with others for the rest of her life.

The first (only because it predates the child's ability to smile) "social" script forms from the multiple sequences of distress-anguish in baby triggering distress-anguish in caregiver, motivating caregiver to relieve distress-anguish in baby hence triggering enjoyment-joy (contentment) in both. In other words, very early on, we begin to learn that people relieve our distress and are a source of enjoyment (contentment). These two social scripts are the foundation of interpersonal relationships and emotional connectedness.

The Final Three Affects

Tomkins postulated that the six affects already described evolved in response to stimulus confusion. They simplified human experience of the surrounding world and enhanced survival ability. The final three affects probably appeared somewhat later in our evolution, but they, too, were in response to problems whose solution was necessary for survival. The first two deal with problems related to hunger drive and are the only affects for which Tomkins did not feel it was necessary to describe a range. Hence, he defined them with single words.

Disgust

This NEGATIVE affect is *inherently punishing.* It provides us some protection when we eat poisonous or rotten food. Obviously, some things that are poisonous do not taste bad or cause a reaction in the stomach that triggers vomiting. However, many things we should not ingest are foul-tasting or caustic to the stomach lining. When this stimulus occurs, disgust is the affect triggered. In *AIC* Vol. I, page 50, Tomkins describes disgust as a "built-in rejection mechanism specifically designed to enable the individual to avoid or eject food."

The actions of the head and face when there is disgust involve *a forward movement of the head, a protrusion of the tongue, and a pushing down of the lower lip.* If the response is very intense, vomiting occurs. I do not know the child in the next picture loaned to me by Don Nathanson. It appears in his book *Shame and Pride.* The disgust on her face is obvious.

While disgust originated simply as an accompaniment for hunger drive, it becomes a powerful force in our lives. For instance, we can be disgusted with the behavior of another person or ourselves or whole groups of people.

Dissmell

This NEGATIVE affect is also *inherently punishing*. It is the only affect which Tomkins felt needed a new word. It is the automatic response we have when we smell something rotten, like sour milk, fresh feces, or decaying organic matter. When the smell stimulus reaches the brain, *the head draws back and away and the upper lip wrinkles*. For instance, if rotten milk triggers dissmell, no matter how hungry or thirsty one is, it is extremely unlikely he or she will drink that milk.

Don Nathanson also loaned the left-hand picture below from his book *Shame and Pride*. The baby on the right is my granddaughter Louisa at age thirteen months. She has just smelled a dirty diaper.

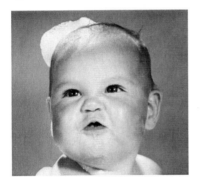

The innate affect dissmell is an important motivating force in the lives of most adults. For example, no one wants others to consider them "a stinker." For this reason, there is a substantial industry in deodorants and deodorizers of all kinds. We become embarrassed if our houses or our bodies stink, and most people go to great lengths to prevent that from happening. Moreover, dissmell is the affect central to the formation of racial and cultural prejudice, a topic of considerable importance that is beyond the scope of this Primer.

Disgust and dissmell evolved as protections against hunger drive. Once triggered, they act as *impediments* to the drive and prevent us from harming ourselves by eating rotten, spoiled, or poisonous substances.

The ninth and final affect we will consider is shame. It also relates to the idea of impediment, but in a way that will initially seem confusing.

Shame-Humiliation

A clear understanding of the exact triggering mechanism for shame is critically important for anyone who wants to penetrate the complexities of human personality, especially the nature of interpersonal relationships. To do so, it will be necessary to suspend temporarily your current notion of what shame is. Since it is not easy to alter a lifelong belief, it might help to pretend I am defining something entirely new, something you have never heard of before. The new definition will not cause you to leave behind all of what you already know, but it will give you a new concept (by a paradigm shift) of how shame originates in all of us. It is important to remember that I am discussing an *innate affect*, the way shame begins in us very early in life.

The process that leads to the triggering of shame will seem somewhat strange at first. Most people—and I include myself in that group—have intuitively resisted believing that what Tomkins described as the trigger for shame-humiliation has anything at all to do with shame as we know it. This is because the usual adult conceptualization of shame is that it means someone did something to "be ashamed of." This, as you will see, turns out to be only one form of shame. The innate affect *shame* evolves into an entire family of emotions of which being "ashamed" is only one member. If you have difficulty—and initially you will—grasping the concept for the basis of innate shame, it is because you are still thinking that the word shame only refers to feeling ashamed of something one said or did. If you can suspend that idea as you read on, I believe you will find this new conceptualization of shame very interesting.

Shame-humiliation was the last of the affects to evolve. As is the case for many aspects of our evolution, shame-humiliation evolved to solve a problem. The best way to describe the problem is to return to the notion of the affect system as a mechanism that provides information about stimulus conditions. Shame-humiliation came after the system already had the ability to register and make us aware of stimulus conditions in the form of five negative affects (fear, distress, anger, disgust, and dissmell), one neutral affect (surprise), and two positive affects (interest and enjoyment). What additional information did the early members of our species need? They did not need more information about the negative affects. Since fear, distress, anger, disgust, and dissmell are inherently punishing, they are already sufficiently motivating for us to do things to get them to stop. Nor did our ancestors need further information about surprise-startle. This affect is neither inherently punishing nor rewarding. It is like a computer's reset button that rapidly clears the system and prepares us for whatever comes next.

The positive affects, however, were another story. Because they were inherently rewarding, once triggered, they motivated behaviors to have them continue. The demand for the evolution of a new information-gathering mechanism arose when something blocked either of the positive affects. Please note carefully that I am not describing a situation where the stimulus conditions triggering interest or enjoyment no longer exist and, as a result, interest and enjoyment come to a natural end. Instead, I mean a situation where stimulus conditions for the triggering of positive affect were still present for our forbearers, but a conflicting stimulus condition arose that blocked the continuation of positive affect.

Here is an example of the difference: Imagine you are waiting in your friend's car while she is in the supermarket. In the playground across the street, playing children trigger your interest and hence your attention. You observe them to be playing a game you have never seen before. The novelty of the game triggers more interest. After several minutes, you figure out the game they are playing. The children keep playing but continually repeat the same actions. The game loses its novelty, and your interest diminishes. Soon there is a natural termination of the stimulus conditions for interest-excitement; that affect simply stops. Because the stimulus has ceased, you are no longer motivated to direct your attention to the game.

It is an entirely different matter, however, if you are still interested in figuring out the game but a large delivery truck blocks your line of sight when it pulls between you and the playground. The truck now impedes your ongoing interest, and you experience a negative feeling. The intensity of the negative feeling is in direct proportion to how interested you were in the game. If you were very interested, then you feel a strong negative feeling that might even motivate you to get out of the car and move to a place where you can see the playground again. As surprising as it may seem, this negative feeling—which, as an adult, you might describe as frustration or anger—Tomkins decided was shame-humiliation.

He believed that we evolved shame-humiliation as information about the stopping of the stimulus condition of ongoing positive affect when we did not want it to stop. This was, and is, critical information for us to have. *Without it, we would not be motivated to take action when we cannot continue with interesting and enjoyable things.* This would be a sad state of affairs. If we were not motivated to pursue our interests when they encounter impediments, most of the discoveries of humanity would not have occurred. Research scientists, professional athletes, great musicians—as well as you and I—have all experienced roadblocks to interest in advancing our knowledge and skills. Shame affect provides the motivating information for the uncovering and removal of impediments to our interests. Shame affect also provides the motivating information for the uncovering and removal of impediments to things we enjoy. Without shame, as unpleasant as it may feel at times, our lives would be completely different and much less fun.

Thus it is easy to understand why such an affect would have evolved and become part of our innate, inborn endowment. Because Tomkins had a remarkable mental ability to coordinate massive amounts of information, including Darwin's theories of evolution, and draw conclusions about our most fundamental nature, he saw that all of an entire family of emotions had a single cause. He identified it as *impediment to ongoing positive affect*. What is more difficult to grasp is why in the world Tomkins decided that the stimulus condition of impediment to ongoing positive affect is the trigger for *shame-humiliation*. The confusion all of us have experienced trying to grasp this arises from a number of different sources. They include the difficult-to-abandon belief that feeling "ashamed" is the only evidence that shame is present; and the fact that from very early on in our lives, to avoid feeling shame, we develop rapidly activated defenses to make us unaware that shame is present. As I mentioned earlier, feeling ashamed is just one of an extensive family of shame emotions, but it is the one—with its milder form embarrassment and its harsher form humiliation—that most people associate with the word "shame."

Earlier, I described the difference between affects, feelings, and emotions. I made the point that emotion results from a mixture of the biology of our affects with our biographies—our life experience with each of the affects. Although this is not the place to go into great detail about the *family of emotions* shame gives birth to, it might help clarify the function of shame affect if I mention a few of them. (See Chapter 1 for a more detailed description of the shame family of emotions.)

When an impediment blocks our interest in something, the resulting shame can feel like any one or more of the following: **frustration** or **disappointment** (I can't do what I want to do); **rejection** (my interest in my lover is blocked because she doesn't want me anymore); **loneliness** (my interest in people being interested in me is blocked because I'm all by myself and cannot find a date); **feeling ashamed** or **embarrassed** (my interest in people seeing me as perfect and loving me is blocked because I said a stupid thing or did something awful, or I have a blemish on my face and everyone will find out); and/or, at its most intensely negative, **mortification** (what happened is so awful that my interest in living is blocked). While the last of these emotions is life-threatening, even it is information that permits us to reevaluate what has happened.

The bodily responses to shame are a *diverting down of the eyes, a slumping to the side of the head as the muscles of the neck go limp, and sometimes the appearance of a blush.* The pictures below are also courtesy of Don Nathanson. The baby on the left is unknown to me but appears to be less than six months old. It is clear from this picture that the affect shame-humiliation is present from an early age. About the picture on the right, Nathanson says in *Shame and Pride*, page 135, "Here shame interferes with this baby's ability to remain interested in the toy. Was the kiss intended to pull the baby out of its slump, or was it the trigger for shame-humiliation?"

In Chapter 5, I utilize Nathanson's **Compass of Shame** formulation to address how the defenses against shame make it virtually invisible to us. For now, I want to encourage you to challenge your current way of perceiving shame by presenting three examples of situations in which the innate affect shame-humiliation is triggered. On reflection, I think you will agree that in each example no one has done anything to be "ashamed of." The first example is one used by Tomkins in *AIC* Vol. II, page 123, and paraphrased by Nathanson in *Shame and Pride*, page 134, as follows:

Recall, asks Tomkins, all those times you have seen an old friend at a distance and waved vigorously to get his or her attention. When that other person gives us the smiling face of recognition, we are rewarded by a surge of pleasure. But occasionally it turns out that we had hailed a stranger, having been fooled by an unexpected resemblance.

The moment we recognize our error something surprising happens to us. Although one might think all we need do is maintain our composure, nod politely, and ask this person to

188 • *the* ART *of* INTIMACY

excuse the intrusion, before we can get the words out of our mouths, something else has taken place. As soon as we have seen the face of the other person, our own head droops. Our eyes are cast down, and, blushing, we become briefly incapable of speech. Sometimes a hand goes unbidden to the mouth as if to prevent further communication, and we feel a surge of confusion.

Here is how affect psychologists view this situation: If the person had been our old friend, there would have been a lovely flow of positive affect between us. There would have been interest in the other person's life intermingled with their interest in ours. There would have been enjoyment at learning the new things happening for each. There would have been positive feelings of shared memories creating an enjoyable few moments together. However, the instant of awareness that we do not know this person acts as an impediment to all the anticipated positive affect. This triggers shame as evidenced by the drooping of the head, the diverting of the eyes, and the blushing, bumbling attempt at speech. I think you would agree that this is a situation where no one did anything shameful or to be ashamed of. Someone has simply made an honest mistake. No one has committed a serious social faux pas. In fact, it would have been more socially inappropriate or "shameful" to ignore someone we thought to be an old friend.

The reaction of the person approaching us in this situation is also noteworthy. They, too, cast their eyes to the side, head drooping in an obvious moment of shame at the instant of awareness that we do not know one another. Has this person done anything socially inappropriate for which they should feel shame? No. In fact, it would have been a social faux pas (shameful behavior) if they had ignored our summons, walking away rather than approaching a smiling person signaling them. The reason this person has shame triggered is that, thinking they were being summoned by somebody they might know, they also had their interest piqued and then blocked at the moment of clear awareness that we are strangers.

Neither person in this imagined scenario has any reason to feel ashamed of their actions. Instead, both have simply experienced the impedance of a potentially positive interaction. Most of us have probably been in such a situation and would be inclined to refer to the mild intensity of the shame triggered as *embarrassment*, an embarrassment we might well chuckle at later in the day, amazed that the stranger looked so much like one of our friends. In other words, the shame triggered by the event would be no big deal. Instead, it is simply information about blockage of positive affect by a normally functioning affect system, information that something we wanted to have and to have more of was withheld from us.

My second example of impediment to positive affect triggering shame recounts a scene familiar to all who have observed small children. As mentioned earlier, novelty is the primary stimulus condition for triggering the affect interest-excitement. No one lives with more novelty than the very young. After they begin to develop a relationship with their caregivers, they have a very natural interest in people. At some point, all normal kids develop a reaction called "stranger anxiety."[6] Conventional knowledge has labeled it such for years. One manifestation of this occurs when a toddler, brimming with interest, approaches a person but suddenly becomes aware that this is someone unfamiliar. The toddler turns away, heading back to mommy or daddy, often to grab hold of a leg and bury their head in the safe place. Since my introduction to affect psychology, I have studied such reactions from a new perspective. I hope you will do the same. Look carefully at the child. He or she has not just buried their head in mommy's leg: the head droops as well, and the eyes are diverted away from the stranger. If you look very carefully at the right moment, you will even see a blush on the face of the child, making it even more obvious that he or she is feeling shame. The caregiver might even say, "She's going through a shy period right now."

I cannot imagine anyone who would argue the case that the child has done something to be ashamed of, or, for that matter, that such a young child even knows yet what it means to be ashamed. So why does s/he have shame? Again, this is a situation where the stimulus condition is that of *impediment to positive affect*. The fact that s/he did not recognize the stranger acts as a blockage or a diminishing of the child's very great interest in people. Furthermore, s/he does not yet have in place scripts for dealing with strangers. After a while, when an "I know what to do with a stranger" script is present, the child might well engage the new person in active play or conversation and have a very positive experience.

The child's shame reaction is another example that from birth we are "hard-wired" to feel bad when something happens to prevent ongoing interest or enjoyment. I think you would agree that this is very useful information, even if it does not feel good. It is somewhat ironic that in

---

6. *Anxiety* is another overly general term that can refer to one or more different affects. At times, it is used to refer to fear, at others distress or shame. Affect psychologists dislike the term because it is so lacking in specificity that its use causes a great deal of misunderstanding in research and interpersonal communication.

order to be aware that we are missing something that feels good we have to feel bad, but it makes sense when you think about it. Would we pay attention to the thing that initially felt good but was then blocked if the feeling that replaced it was another good feeling? I do not think so. Evolution has provided us with a very effective mechanism. I like to think of the problems caused by shame—and there are many—as side effects of its function, just as the many problems caused by our immune system such as allergies, lupus, or rheumatoid arthritis are side effects of its function gone awry.

The third example and final example of a situation where shame is triggered but no one has done anything shameful involves two lovers. Imagine one especially beautiful day in spring that finds one of the lovers in a romantic mood, experiencing sexual interest-excitement at the thought of an evening's tryst. When the lovers finally meet at the end of the day, the excited lover rushes to the other and makes very clear the desire for an evening filled with sexual pleasure. The other admits to having felt the same sexual feelings earlier in the day but adds that for the last hour or two s/he has had chills and nausea. As the first lover peers carefully into the face of the beloved, it is obvious from the pale, washed-out visage that there is absolutely not going to be any sexual activity that night—the beloved has the flu. Along with this realization comes a brief moment of a negative feeling in the first lover, who might describe it as a feeling of rejection, even though the second lover has done nothing of the sort. This feeling is the result of shame because the one lover's flu is an impediment to the other lover's sexual interest-excitement.

There was no actual rejection of the other by the sick lover, nor did the feeling of rejection stem from any sexual hang-ups between the two. It was simply a matter of the new, unexpected information (the flu) acting as an impediment to positive affect triggering shame. For true lovers, the moment would quickly pass. Interest in the well-being of the other, and perhaps the preparation of a large pot of chicken soup, would rapidly replace the sexual interest-excitement of the first lover. Any feelings of rejection would soon be forgotten and lead to no future repercussions. Perhaps the two would even have a good laugh later on about what a great evening it would have been if only the flu had not intervened.

I suspect that the three examples above have not fully convinced you that shame is more than just feeling ashamed. If your interest in learning more about shame and the shame family of emotions has been stimulated, I again suggest you read Nathanson's in-depth exploration of the topic in *Shame and Pride*. However, I hope you have at least begun to consider that shame is an innate biological mechanism, the only purpose of which is to make us aware of impediment to positive affect. It seems only logical that we would have evolved a mechanism to serve this function. Without the information that something is preventing us from feeling good, we would be unable to either achieve or maintain a healthy balance between positive and negative emotion.

Partial Summary of Affect System Function

1. Part of normal brain function evolved to reduce stimulus confusion.
2. Nothing becomes conscious unless an affect is triggered first.
3. A specific stimulus condition or pattern triggers each affect.
4. Affect is information about stimulus conditions.
5. Positive affect is inherently rewarding, negative affect inherently punishing.

Central Blueprint for Motivation

One very important feature of having an affect system with inherently rewarding and punishing affects, combined with our capacity to analyze things, our ability to remember things, and our ability to create mental (not visual) images of what we want, is that our brain has evolved a blueprint for motivation. This blueprint contains four rules that work together like four sections in an orchestra, one sometimes more prominent than the others, depending on circumstances, but all always playing. They are:

1. Positive affect should be maximized,
2. Negative affect should be minimized,
3. Affect inhibition should be minimized, and
4. The power to maximize positive affect, to minimize negative affect, to minimize the inhibition of affect should be maximized.

Appendix II

BIBLIOGRAPHY

Suggestions for General Reading

Catherall, Don R. *Emotional Safety: Viewing Couples Through the Lens of Affect*. New York, Routledge, 2007.

Dilley, R.B. *In a Moment's Notice: A Psychologist's Journey with Breast Cancer*. 2010.

Holinger, P.C., and K. Doner. *What Babies Say Before They Can Talk*. New York: Fireside (Simon & Schuster), 2003.

Hutchison, K. *Walking After Midnight*. Oakland, CA: New Harbinger, 2006.

Nathanson, D.L. *Shame and Pride: Affect, Sex, and the Birth of the Self*. New York: Norton, 1992

Schnarch, D. *Passionate Marriage*. New York: Norton, 1997.

Wright, J. *The Art of Attention: Chronicles of an Imagery-Oriented Psychotherapist*. Victoria, BC: Trafford, 2005.

Suggestions for Professionals

Brown, N., and E. Amatea. *Love and Intimate Relationships: Journeys of the Heart*. Philadelphia, Bruner-Mazel, 2000.

Demos, E.V. *Exploring Affect: The Selected Writings of Silvan S. Tomkins*. Cambridge, England, New York, and Paris: Cambridge University Press, 1995.

Holinger, P.C., "Winnicott, Tomkins, and the Psychology of Affect." *Clinical Social Work Journal*, 37:155–162, 2009.

Kaufman, G. *Shame: The Power of Caring* (2d ed.). Cambridge, MA: Schenkman Books, 1985.

——. and L. Raphael. *Coming Out of Shame: Transforming Gay and Lesbian Lives*. New York: Doubleday, 1996.

Kelly, V.C. "Affect and the Redefinition of Intimacy." In Nathanson, D.L. (ed.). *Knowing Feeling: Affect, Script, and Psychotherapy*. New York: Norton, 1996. p. 55–104.

Schnarch, D. *Constructing the Sexual Crucible: An Integration of Sexual and Marital Therapy*. New York: Norton, 1991.

Schneider, C. *Shame, Exposure and Privacy*. Boston, MA: Beacon, 1977.

Stern, D. *The Interpersonal World of the Infant: A View from Psychoanalysis and Developmental Psychology*. New York: Basic Books, 1985.

Tomkins, S. *Affect/Imagery/Consciousness*. Vol. I: *The Positive Affects*. New York: Springer, 1962.

——. *Affect/Imagery/Consciousness*. Vol. II: *The Negative Affects*. New York: Springer, 1963.

——. *Affect/Imagery/Consciousness*. Vol. III: *The Negative Affects: Anger and Fear*. New York: Springer, 1991.

——. *Affect/Imagery/Consciousness*. Vol. IV: *Cognition: Duplication and Transformation of Information*. New York: Springer, 1992.

——. *Affect/Imagery/Consciousness: The Complete Edition*. Two-volume boxed set. New York: Springer, 2008.